Praise for *Inside Islam* and *Inside Israel*

"*Inside Islam* . . . reminds us how vital it is for Americans to have a greater understanding of the international environment. The collection is a good introduction not just to the variety of religious experience in the Muslim world, but also to the political dynamics that help fuel fundamentalist hatred of the West in general and of the United States above all."

—*The Los Angeles Times*

"This compilation of essays and book excerpts . . . offers a timely and valuable introduction to the multifaceted world of Islam."

—*Publishers Weekly* on *Inside Islam* [Starred Review]

"Standout essays in this essential book."

—*O, The Oprah Magazine* on *Inside Islam*

"A timely gathering of articles and essays on a rapidly expanding influential faith."

—*Kirkus Reviews* on *Inside Islam*

"Deeper introductions to Islam exist, but none has the quality of writing collected here. . . . Readers interested in Islam will treasure this accessible collection."

—*Booklist* on *Inside Islam* [Featured Review]

"Islam will continue to have a profound effect on Americans, and every thinking person should have a fundamental understanding of Muslim views. *Inside Islam* is a suitable place to begin. . . . The book provides a solid foundation for understanding this complex society."

—*Rocky Mountain News*

"This book provides valuable reading to those who seriously seek to understand current world events."

—*The Tampa Tribune* on *Inside Islam*

"*Inside Islam* is full of valuable and provocative perspectives. . . . This book is one way to get started learning about the many sides of Islam."

—*Body & Soul*

"[An] eminently readable collection."

—*The Jerusalem Post* on *Inside Israel*

INSIDE IRAQ

Books by John Miller and Aaron Kenedi

Inside Islam

Inside Israel

Where Inspiration Lives

God's Breath: Sacred Scriptures of the World

Muhammad Ali: Ringside

Revolution: Faces of Change

San Francisco Stories

Legends: Women Who Have Changed the World

INSIDE IRAQ

THE HISTORY, THE PEOPLE, AND THE MODERN CONFLICTS OF THE WORLD'S LEAST UNDERSTOOD LAND

Edited by John Miller and Aaron Kenedi

Introduction by David Rose

MARLOWE & COMPANY
NEW YORK

INSIDE IRAQ: *The History, the People, and the Modern Conflicts of the World's Least Understood Land*

Published by Marlowe & Company
An Imprint of Avalon Publishing Group Incorporated
161 William Street, 16th Floor
New York, NY 10038

Editor's note: Changes for consistency have been made to the essays in this book.

Cover and interior design: Miller Media
Cover photograph: © Peter Turnley/Corbis
Permissions research: Shawneric Hachey
Proofreading and copyediting: Mimi Kusch

Library of Congress Cataloging-in-Publication Data

Inside Iraq: the history, the people, and the modern conflicts of the world's least understood land / edited by John Miller and Aaron Kenedi; introduction by David Rose.
p. cm.
Includes bibliographical references (p.) and index.
ISBN 1-56924-480-4
1. Iraq—History—1958- 2. Hussein, Saddam, 1937- I. Miller, John, 1959- II. Kenedi, Aaron

DS79.65.I56 2003
956.704—dc21

2003041295

9 8 7 6 5 4 3 2 1

Printed in the United States of America
Distributed by Publishers Group West

Special thanks to
Amy Rennert
and Matthew Lore

Contents

THE CONFLICTS

DAVID ROSE

Introduction

IRAQ, THE MODERN NAME for Mesopotamia, the land between the rivers Tigris and Euphrates, is where civilization started. And there, so some of the more outspoken western critics of going to war with the regime of Saddam Hussein sometimes seem to be arguing, is where it may soon be coming to an end.

At the time of writing, in the third week of December 2002, the struggle within the U.S. administration of George W. Bush, which has been waged almost continuously since the terrorist attacks of September 2001, appears finely balanced. The hawks, gathered mainly in the Pentagon and in the office of Vice President Dick Cheney, still speak confidently about the cocktail parties to come after liberation in Baghdad's premier hotel, the Al Rashid. The State Department's doves continue to insist that war both should and can be avoided, and that the recently returned United Nations weapons inspectors can nullify Saddam's threat to his neighbors without the need for regime change through force. Each side in this debate has found a sounding board in the international media, where the question of Iraq has overwhelmingly dominated coverage and comment throughout the year now almost past. Few wars in history—if war does indeed lie at the end of this grueling political road—can have been so widely and lengthily trailed, debated, and agonized over in advance.

As the essays in this volume demonstrate in disparate ways, the fierceness of this debate is entirely appropriate. Milton Viorst's view of the dignity and resilience of Baghdad reveals a city strangely at peace with itself in times of war. It is a city that seems to have been built with one main purpose: to *survive*. But as Michael Kelly and Paul William Roberts explore Iraq's culture, they reveal a country struggling not just to survive, but to evolve into the new world under the constant specter of war, guided by a unique blend of cryptic political policy and old-fashioned tyranny.

Since the time of the prophet Abraham, the importance of Iraq has been out of all proportion to its geographical size. It was where writing, bureaucracy, and the rule of law were invented and the site of the city of Babylon, from which the emperor Nebuchadnezzar—to whom Saddam often likes to be compared—three thousand years ago invaded and smashed the first Jewish state. Seventeen hundred years later, the successive martyrdoms of Muhammad's son-in-law Ali and grandson Hussein spawned the Shiite branch of Islam, and so gave Iraq its holiest shrines; not much later Baghdad became the seat of Sunni civilization's highwater mark, the Abbasid caliphate. Now, in the twenty-first century, the outcome of events in Mesopotamia may be still more significant, to both the Middle East and the wider world.

Saddam's regime is something unique: a form of totalitarian gangsterism, in which all the tools of Stalinist repression at its worst have been turned to serve not an ideology, but a single despotic family. His murderous depredations against his own people, from the nerve-gassing of the Kurds of Halabja to the assassinations of his father-in-law and two sons-in-law, need no further exposition here. Yet in the place of this charnel house of tyranny, many believe there is a genuine possibility of establishing a wholly different kind of government. The prospect of Iraq as a future beacon of democratic values does not figure high in President Bush's rhetoric, while those who oppose a military ouster have characterized the notion as wholly fanciful. In the words of Nicholas D. Kristof of the *New York Times*, it is but "a pipe dream, a marketing ploy to sell a war," and the best Iraqis can hope for is "Saddam lite," a merely less brutal dictator. But it is this democratic idea—not, as some allege, the prospect of cheaper oil supplies—that underlies the thinking and drives the passion of those who make the hawkish case. Richard Perle, assistant defense secretary under President Reagan, now the chairman of the Pentagon's Policy Board, told me that in regime change in Iraq, he sees an opportunity as great as that which Reagan took in the early 1980s, when he dared to call the Soviet Empire "evil" and set in train the measures which led to its undoing.

A more or less democratic Iraq might, he said, initiate a "benign domino effect," in which all or most of the Arab tyrannies now in power would slowly give way to democracy, just as the dictatorships of Latin America did in the 1980s and 1990s. While Perle and the Defense Deputy Secretary, Paul Wolfowitz, are the most visible advocates of this position, its intellectual father is Bernard Lewis, emeritus professor of near eastern studies at Princeton, associate of Vice President Dick Cheney, and author of more than two dozen books on the history of the Middle East. Lewis is under no illusions about the difficulty of rebuilding a semblance of civil society in Saddam's shattered Iraq. Yet if there is one Arab country that might begin to illuminate the way toward a third, democratic model between the false dichotomy of fundamentalist or secular tyranny, Lewis told me, it is Iraq.

There was a time in his own academic career, he recalled, when its graduate students had quite clearly emerged from the best educational system in the Middle East, and under the Hashemites, who ruled from 1921 until the first military coup in 1958, Iraq moved some distance towards secular, constitutional monarchy. Meanwhile, there was the example of Turkey, "which proves two things—that establishing democracy in the Middle East is very difficult, and that it *is* possible."

Mesopotamia's near future may be historically significant in another way.

After the end of the cold war, America spent most of a decade trying hard not to confront the deeper meaning and heavier responsibilities that sole, unchallenged, superpower status had conferred. The military interventions it and its allies made in Somalia, Bosnia, Kosovo, and Afghanistan arose in response to immediate crisis. They were not made, and not justified, in terms of an emerging global *imperium*.

To be sure, surrounding Iraq too is an aura of crisis, of immediacy: its possession of weapons of mass destruction, and what I believe to be its heavy involvement with the Al Qaeda terrorists who perpetrated the attacks of September 2001. At the same time, Iraq has had these weapons, and these terrorist links, for many years, just as it has carried out human rights violations on an epic scale. Effecting regime change in Baghdad—what the Iraqi opposition leader Ahmad Chalabi calls "a war *for* Iraq" may come, in time, to be seen in part as the first proactive intervention of a new kind, in pursuit not of treasure but of greater human decency.

—DAVID ROSE
OXFORD, ENGLAND
DECEMBER 2002

THE HISTORY

MILTON VIORST

The View From Mustansiriyah

BAGHDAD, IN WAR, SEEMS remarkably at peace with itself. No tanks are parked at the intersections, as there are in so many Arab cities; there are no sandbagged kiosks in which armed soldiers sit guarding public buildings. Iraqi soldiers walking the streets wear a home-for-the-weekend look rather than weapons on their shoulders Baghdad is a gregarious city, and gritty enough to pay no attention to the hammering of the Iranian Army a hundred miles or so to the east. Unlike the street life of other Arab cities, which tends to end when the sun goes down, Baghdad's only then begins. I visited the city this summer, when the temperature reached 110 or even 115 degrees every afternoon,

MILTON VIORST *is a longtime Middle Eastern correspondent for* The New Yorker. *He has written numerous books about the region including* In the Shadow of the Prophet *and* Sandcastles; *this excerpt is from his 1991* Report from Baghdad.

keeping most Baghdadis hidden from midday to early evening. At about six, as the heat abated, people began to crowd the streets and marketplaces, and to fill the cafés. What I remember is not air-raid sirens and sonic booms but parents playing with their children in the parks after dark, and couples strolling on the promenade along the Tigris. At midnight, the downtown night clubs were just getting busy, while in the restaurants young men sat in groups over beer or soft drinks. War or no war, Baghdad felt safer to me than Times Square. It is a more vibrant city than Damascus or Cairo, its great Arab rivals, and it has made a calculated decision to let the war disturb its composure as little as possible.

The scene, of course, changes from one district to the next in Baghdad, as it does in other great cities. Though modern in most respects, with wide boulevards and clean water and push-button phones, Baghdad is nonetheless a collection of highly diverse neighborhoods. Once a cluster of buildings on the riverbank, it now extends a dozen miles from north to south along the serpentine turns of the Tigris, and a half-dozen miles to east and west. Its population, which was a hundred and forty thousand in 1900, has soared to four million, more than a quarter of the country's total. In growing, Baghdad reached out not just to pave farmland but to swallow towns and villages with their own distinct identity. Much of the space between these old towns and villages now contains agglomerations of high-rise apartment buildings—urban scapes so familiar to the eye that they could belong to almost any city anywhere. But the communities themselves have never been completely digested, and as neighborhoods they retain not only their historical names but their unique character. Together, they make of the city a mosaic of Iraqi history, the record of a people in the era of Islam.

In 762, the Caliph al-Mansur, of the Abbasid dynasty—the title "caliph" signifies successor to the Prophet Muhammad, and thus Islam's supreme authority, both temporal and spiritual—laid the first brick of his new imperial capital on the Tigris. In doing so, he transferred the center of Arab power from the desert cities of Damascus and Medina (Cairo did not yet exist) to the fertile plain between the Tigris and the Euphrates—known as Mesopotamia—a place already rich in history. The Sumerians had flourished in Mesopotamia. Hammurabi and Nebuchadnezzar had reigned in Babylon, fifty miles to the south of Baghdad, and Alexander the Great had died there. The Persians had governed a vast empire from nearby Ctesiphon, from which the Arabs drove them in 687, in a battle that Iraqis today call the opening shot of a war that has still not ended. The Abbasids, in establishing themselves in Baghdad, turned the geographical perspective of the Arabs eastward; in time, Islamic armies would spread the faith to the Ganges, and Islamic mariners would make converts as far away as the Pacific Islands.

No less important, the Abbasid decision to settle on the Tigris exposed the Arab world to Persia's rich artistic and literary culture. Even while Abbasid armies continued to advance, the influence of Persian culture transferred dominance among the Arabs from the austere and ardent warriors of Islam to a new class of merchants, craftsmen, and scholars. By the ninth century, Baghdad was celebrated the world over for its intellectual and artistic creativity and the Abbasid caliph Harun al-Rashid, like Charlemagne of France, was recognized as the head of a great world empire. Indeed, had a visitor from Mars descended in those days he would surely have judged the Abbasids' the more powerful and more cultured civilization. Except for a sojourn of fifty-three years in Samarra, the Abbasid dynasty reigned in Baghdad for five centuries, though its imperium, enfeebled by usurpers from inside and out, was much shorter-lived. In 1258, invading Mongols, encountering little resistance, slaughtered the last of the ruling caliphs. And so the city slipped into oblivion, to play no significant role in world affairs until the present era.

Unfortunately, little is left in Baghdad to remind one of the Abbasid glory, though only part of the blame can be laid on the Mongols or the plunderers who followed them. The fault is chiefly nature's: Mesopotamia is not blessed with stone. The only abundant native building material is mud, and until recently nearly every structure—whether dwelling, mosque, palace, city wall, gate, or market—was constructed of mud formed into bricks and laid out in the sun to bake. As a consequence, Iraq's cities and towns exhibit a bland sameness, a dull beige uniformity that blends into the general flat terrain, giving little pleasure to the eye.

It is true that as far back as Babylonian times builders knew how to improve on the basic material. By firing the brick in kilns, they could make it nearly as durable a. stone. Surviving fragments provide evidence that the Babylonians made aesthetic use of fired brick to create variety in design, and though Babylon was laid waste long ago, even today nearby towns contain handsome walls made of bricks pilfered from the imperial ruins. The problem for builders through the centuries, however, was that they needed fuel for their kilns, and until our own times no one knew that beneath the surface of the soil was a highly combustible substance in almost limitless quantity. Today, throughout Iraq, kilns much like those of two or three millennia ago are fuelled by oil. But before oil the only known fuel was wood, and it had to be imported from India or Lebanon or Africa. Architects knew the principles of the dome and the arch, and employed such forms in public buildings; however, since they found it more economical to use wood as a building material than as a fuel, they preferred timbered roofs to domed or arched roofs of fired brick. Thus, over the years, wood became commonplace, both structurally and ornamentally, in Baghdad's buildings. But posterity was the loser, since termites ate the wood and weather eroded the mud walls. The result is that, apart from a few noble structures of fire brick, hardly anything in the city is more than a century old.

Still, Baghdad has never fully lost its Abbasid flavor. The core of the capital a thousand years ago—a community called Rusafa, which hugs the east bank of the Tigris along a straight stretch of a mile or two between sharp curves to the north and west—remains the core today. This was not the city's original site, which was a fortress built by al-Mansur in the eighth century—the so-called Round City. The Abbasids, after their stay in Samarra, chose not to return to the Round City; their second settlement was at Rusafa. Today, it is a warren of human habitations clustered around a few buildings constructed in the thirteenth century, just before the Mongol conquest. In the centuries that followed, the face of the city hardly changed. The historian Philip K. Hitti notes in his book *Capital Cities of Arab Islam* that a map sketched by a French merchant named Tavernier, who visited Baghdad in 1651, barely differs from a map drawn by the British when they seized the city from the Ottoman Turks, in 1917.

The hub of the Rusafa quarter is the Mustansiriyah, built in 1234 as a university for studies in mathematics, astronomy, medicine, and—especially—Islamic jurisprudence. The main gate is elaborately decorated with calligraphy and geometric designs, but the real artistic emphasis was placed on the interior. Embracing a courtyard the size of a football field, the four inside walls are each centered on a two-story arch symbolizing one of the four major schools of Islamic law. From the high arches run two tiers of single-story arched galleries, behind which are lecture halls, small chambers designed for student quarters, and a large library. Local lore has it that when the Mongol hordes swarmed into the city, Hulagu, their chief, ordered all the books in the Mustansiriyah library thrown into the Tigris, which for days ran black from the ink. But even Hulagu could not destroy the Mustansiriyah's two-foot-thick fired-brick walls, and when Baghdad passed under Ottoman rule, in the early seventeenth century, the building was put to use variously as a secondary school, an inn, a military academy, a hospital, and an army barracks. Currently, the government's Department of Antiquities is completing an effort to return it to its original state.

Surrounding the Mustansiriyah are ancient mosques, their domes and minarets visible from within the courtyard. The chant of the muezzins (amplified these days by loudspeakers) is audible even inside the student chambers. Just to the Mustansiriyah's north lies the Abbasid palace; historians are unsure which caliph built it. The design is remarkable; its three-foot-thick walls are pierced by vertical shafts that capture breezes from the roof and dispatch them below; and its vaulted galleries, highly ornamented on both ceilings and facade, rise thirty feet from the level of the huge courtyard, providing sun-free access to any part of the building. Even on the most fiercely hot days its chambers are cool, and outside is a promenade for strolling in pleasant weather. The Turks turned it into a fortress during their three-hundred-year occupation, but apart from building an addition to house their cannon they did no serious damage. The palace looks downstream over the Tigris to the souk—the market area—which lies just beyond the Mustansiriyah's south wall.

From the Mustansiriyah's roof, the souk appears to exist in a time warp. One has a clear view of a square mile of commerce: of small domes built by the Turks to cover many of the stalls, and of crumbling plaster pillars, with eroded capitals, which fix the market's boundaries. There are tattered awnings layered with dust, which appear to have provided shade for centuries, and corrugated-metal sheets—contemporary technology's unsightly contribution to keeping out the sun; beneath them the crowds move in and out. Many of the men are Egyptian; a half-million or so Egyptians were recruited to replace the Iraqis mobilized for the war. Generally, they pass unnoticed, but Egyptians who labor in Iraqi fields are mostly peasants, and favor their native dress—the turban and the long-skirted *jallabiyah*. With the Iraqi women, who wear the traditional black *abayah*, they impart to the souk an exotic, medieval flavor.

Inside the souk, the passageways are dark and narrow, their floors damp and dirty. The shops, each usually tended by a single proprietor, are generally clustered in specialized sections, much like a department store—stationery, toiletries, plumbing supplies, shoes, fruit, bolts of fabric for men's suits, jewelry, housewares. There is a ladies'-underwear souk, past which the men are expected to hurry discreetly, and a doctors' and dentists' souk. My favorite is the spice souk, where open burlap bags display golden shades of brown and emit rich and pungent odors. There is also a gold souk, where products are weighed, then sold according to the international price, with little or no bargaining. The customers are almost all women, who hoard their dinars to buy gold as an insurance policy in a male-dominated culture, and pass it on to their daughters, usually in the form of a dowry.

Sometimes the images in the souk seem incongruous indeed: a Bedouin woman wrapped in black, her leathery face tattooed on forehead and cheek, gently fondling a piece of white lace; a shopkeeper wearing a *dishdashah*, the native gown, tracking his inventory of men's shirts and ties on a computer. On a walk through the souk one morning, I entered what appeared to be a remnant of an Ottoman building, now a café, where old men were passing the day drinking tea and smoking a local tobacco through elaborate pipes called narghiles. Electric fans spun overhead, and in one corner a primitive air-conditioner whirred. I sat down at an unwashed table, and an Egyptian waiter served me, unasked, a glass of sweet, hot tea and another of cold water. When he realized that I was not going to drink the water, he poured it on the floor, and the heat evaporated it within a few seconds. Most of the smokers wore a *sayah*, a cross-cultural outfit consisting of a suit jacket and tieless shirt worn over a floor-length skirt and completed by a *kufiyah* and *agal*, the headdress made famous by Yasir Arafat. Like the men who were wearing it, the *sayah* is a product of the British colonial age; no young Iraqi would be caught dead in such a costume.

Parallel to the souk, and set back a hundred yards or so from the Tigris, is the celebrated Rashid Street, Baghdad's first modern thoroughfare and still its most captivating. Anticipating the new era, the Ottomans began its construction in 1915, the year the railroad arrived from the Bosporus. Their aim was to replace a labyrinth of dark, impenetrable alleys with a straight street, wide enough for two motor vehicles to pass. Completed by the British after the First World War, it became a street of arcades sheltering tiny shops and cafés, and though its builders indulged in a wide range of designs, its entire length was shaded by overhanging balconies. Initially called New Street, it was renamed in 1921, on the occasion of the founding of the Hashemite kingdom—the first Iraqi government in seven hundred years. Its name commemorates Harun, the greatest of the Abbasid caliphs, whose honorific title, al-Rashid, means "follower of the right path." In the years since, Baghdad has acquired busier, prettier, more stylish thoroughfares. But, as the city's grand old avenue, Rashid Street has attracted banks and schools and museums, and though a trifle shabby, it remains the spine of the modern city.

Adjacent to Rashid Street, a web of narrow, largely dilapidated passageways evoke Baghdad's bourgeois world of a century or more ago. Typically, Baghdadi homes were built around courtyards, an arrangement that provided both privacy and protection from the sun. Squeezed against their neighbors along alleys no wider than a laden donkey, these houses were as cool as the climate allowed. Many were built with a screened balcony called a *shanashil,* which further darkened the street below. The *shanashil* is the source of much Baghdadi legend. Often elaborately adorned with carved or paneled wood, it has produced countless tales of across-the-street embraces of young lovers, of women collecting gossip while watching the passersby. Beautiful *shanashil* are still visible in some of Baghdad's old quarters, but most of the old houses—apart from a handful serving as museums—are in serious disrepair. Indeed, it is difficult to find traditional Baghdad houses still in use. Sealed off from the street, the traditional house functioned in an atmosphere of seclusion, being divided into the *diwankhanah*, a section reserved for the men and their guests, and the *haram*, the domain of the women and children. The men took their meals together, seated on the floor and served by the women; family ceremonies in which both men and women participated were rare. Rugs and cushions were normally the only furnishings, since the style of eating left little use for tables and the style of sleeping left even less use for beds. Family members slept wherever the search for comfort might lead. Carrying their mattresses with them, they moved to the roof on hot nights, to the inner rooms in winter, to the courtyard in the spring, and to rooms off the courtyard, or even to vaulted basements, to nap in the middle of a stifling summer day. Scholars attribute these practices to Baghdad's Bedouin heritage, and though that heritage fades further with each generation, even modern Baghdadi women, when at home, tend to remain inaccessible to men. Yet this custom, too, is dying out as Baghdadis move into modern single-family homes and apartments, in which the climate is defeated by central heating and air-conditioning and limitations of space preclude a definable *haram*.

More publicly than the Baghdad home, lively and racy Abu Nuwas Street is an index of how much Baghdad's ways have changed. Appropriately, it is named for Harun al-Rashid's favorite poet—a bon vivant and composer of erotic, bacchanalian songs who was the son of a Persian washerwoman. Just as Rashid Street was the city's response to the invasion of the motorcar, Abu Nuwas Street—which begins at the Jumhouriyah Bridge, where Rashid Street ends—was its response to the invasion of Western secular values. In the parks that run between Abu Nuwas and the Tigris, young men and women have been known to kiss. In spacious outdoor cafés, men of diverse ages, and even a few women, sit beneath strings of bare lightbulbs drinking not just tea and soft drinks but whiskey and beer until the morning hours. While American rock or the atonal music of the Arabs blares from the loudspeakers, the patrons read, converse boisterously, or play dominoes and backgammon. The street is also celebrated for its open-air restaurants—colorful establishments with roofs of straw matting attached to the branches of trees, wood fires in the center of the floor, and tile tubs in which huge fish swim while waiting to be scooped up in the proprietor's net. The restaurants are expensive, but the fish—cooked in a style known as *mazgouf*—have been called the finest delicacy in town. Even more than for its cafés and restaurants, however, Abu Nuwas has won fame for its night clubs, which, nestled among small bars and dingy hotels on the shabby east side of the street, seem the most fascinatingly disreputable in Baghdad. Though by Western standards the street is tame, by Islamic standards it is naughty—far naughtier than anything on public display in Cairo or Damascus—and for that the Baghdadis love it. On Abu Nuwas, the mosque seems far away.

The tug-of-war between the secularism embodied by Abu Nuwas Street and the religious values of Islam is the central issue that the Middle East faces today. For most Arabs, it supersedes in importance even the long, obsessive struggle with Israel. It is at the heart of the war being fought against Iran on Iraq's eastern frontier, the outcome of which will determine the shape that Iraqi society will assume in the decades to come. President Saddam Hussein and his Baath Party, whose political control of the country is uncontested, have made clear that their first priority is to forge a nation based on secular principles; yet, as every Iraqi knows, the tricks played by history make the conflict between secularism and religion somewhat more complex in Iraq than anywhere else in the Arab world.

Iraq's Arabs, save for the small percentage who are Christian, are divided between the rival branches of Islam—Sunnism and Shiism—with the Shiites constituting a significant majority. The differences between Sunnis and Shiites began thirteen hundred years ago, with a doctrinal split that even then carried political implications. Two rival parties sought to succeed Muhammad—one led by the Umayyads, an aristocratic family of Mecca, and the other by Ali, the Prophet's son-in-law. The Shiites favored Ali, on the ground that keeping the caliphate in the Prophet's family assured spiritual purity, and when Ali was murdered, in 661, the Shiites contended that the right of succession passed to his sons. They lost the battle over succession and became perennial dissenters—a circumstance of particular significance in Iraq, whose neighbor and historical enemy, Iran, has become Islam's leading Shiite nation. The Ottomans, during their three centuries of occupation, distrusted Iraq's Shiites, who were presumed to have interests in common with Iran, and they let the local Sunnis run the country. As much as anything, the Sunnis' long experience as the Iraqi ruling class explains why they tend to be more worldly, more attracted to power, less apprehensive of change, and less ardent in religious practice than the Shiites.

It is particularly exciting to observe these two subcultures on a Thursday evening, when Baghdad is at its most animated. Though Islam does not recognize a Sabbath, in the sense of a day endowed with a special holiness, the Arabs generally take Friday as a day of rest and contemplation. But Baghdadis tend to be less reverent than other Arabs, and, knowing they can sleep late on Friday, they set Thursday evening aside for frolic. Kadhimiyah, the city's bastion of traditional Shiism, bursts with people and light on Thursday night. About five mules upriver from the Mustansiriyah, Kadhimiyah grew as a town around a cemetery for the Quraysh, the Prophet's clan, predating Rusafa by more than a century. The burial place of two important Shiite imams, it has served from its earliest days as a place of religious devotion, and during the Persian occupation of the sixteenth century an elaborate mosque was built there. With two huge domes and four minarets all coated in gold leaf, the mosque remains a Shiite shrine, dominating Kadhimiyah today. Surrounded on two sides by a souk, whose alleys contain some of Baghdad's most beautiful (albeit sadly decrepit) *shanashils*, the Kadhimiyah mosque is a center of nearly ceaseless human activity. The courtyard behind the mosque's outer walls serves the function of a city park. On a Thursday night in the summer, under green neon lights glowing from the minarets and strings of flashing bulbs hung between the domes, with water soaring from an illuminated fountain in the public square, everyone in the ancient town seems to be relaxing in the courtyard of the mosque or promenading on the adjacent streets.

The Shiite women make fuller use of the mosque than the men, who appear content to kneel and pray and then move on. Dressed uniformly in black *abayahs*, the women I saw in the courtyard looked worn from overwork, bad diet, and poverty. Many were veiled, and those who were not, when they noticed me looking at them, reproachfully raised black scarves to their eyes, momentarily concealing their bad teeth and their tattoos. Nursing babies and surrounded by children, they gossiped in alcoves built into the inner side of the courtyard wall, or rested their backs against the marble sides of the mosque itself. They smoked, drank water from thermos jugs, dozed. Some spread blankets on the courtyard pavement and picnicked with their families, eating chicken and flat bread and watermelon, and leaving behind the remains to be swept up later—often much later—by mosque attendants. The women also took charge of commerce at the mosque. Squatting cone-shaped on straw mats in front of the main gate, they sold nuts and candy, balloons, soft drinks, and hot tea. A few held out their hands to beg for coins, and seemed to do as well as those who were in business.

The women who scrolled in the souk and on the streets around the mosque appeared to be of a different generation. Obviously healthier, they carried themselves more stylishly, even when they were leading children. They had no tattoos. Although they, too, wore *abayahs*, they draped them loosely around their bodies, as if fulfilling a duty; colorful dresses and jewelry were visible underneath. Rather often, they showed high heels and slim ankles below their hemlines, and, unlike the women in the mosque courtyard, they made no effort to cover their faces. Many wore lipstick and eye makeup. Though they tended to stroll in groups of two or three, a few walked with men, but rarely arm in arm, and never hand in hand. Juxtaposed against one another in the crowded souk, the women in their *abayahs* and the men in their white shirts formed a checkered pattern of black and white. The scene, though not quite gay, was far from forbidding. The crowd moved at a window-shopping pace, but—except in the gold souk—the Kadhimiyah merchants offered little beyond necessities to look at. From what I could see, the people of Kadhimiyah that night were most interested in looking at one another.

The objective seemed to be the same in al-Mansur, although the atmosphere was much different. Across town from Kadhimiyah, a half hour away by taxi, al-Mansur is an upper-middle-class neighborhood, and it is predominately Sunni. It is named for the Abbasid caliph who founded Baghdad, and contains embassies, several government ministries, a racetrack, elegant houses of contemporary design, and rather little history. The mosques that I saw were short of patrons, and the chant of the muezzin was lost in the din of traffic. Al-Mansur, though hardly a rival to Paris or Rome, is the only section of Baghdad that might lay claim to being chic. Because of the war, imports of consumer items are rare; nonetheless, its shops of locally manufactured men's and women's clothes make an effort to join the current of international style, and there are even boutiques offering snappy outfits for children. Al-Mansur has art galleries and video stores and, I believe, the only shops in the city that sell running shoes and bathing suits (though no bikinis). On my Thursday-night visit, the principal avenue was bumper to bumper with Toyotas and Brazilian-made Volkswagens—Iraq's most popular cars. Driving many of them were young men, who tooted their horns, waved to friends, and scanned the sidewalks for girls. As in Kadhimiyah, the sidewalks were so tightly packed that it was hard to pass, but there was not an *abayah* in sight. A few Saudis in white robes strolled by; everyone else was in Western dress. Well-groomed young parents pushed strollers. Soldiers on leave looked crisp in their khakis and olives. What appeared to be the smart set hurried by—men and women together, perhaps on their way to dinner in one or another of the city's private clubs. Formal restaurants on the avenue served whiskey and beer and a full menu of the local specialties, and small cafés cooked kebabs on open grills. But the neighborhood favorites were clearly the three or four fast-food establishments—copies of McDonald's down to imitative names, with bills of fare posted above the counters in English as well as in Arabic. On the sidewalk in front of these places loitered teenage boys and girls, smoking, sipping soft drinks from paper cups, and flirting.

As if the Sunni-Shiite rivalry were not enough to sustain Iraq's long-standing reputation for being difficult to govern, the regime must make its peace with the country's three million Kurds. Although the great majority are Sunni Muslims, the Kurds are a group of different ethnic and cultural background from that of the Arabs. Speaking their own language, they inhabit the hill country in the northeast, and identify themselves as belonging to a people who occupy a large contiguous area that crosses from Iraq into Iran, Turkey, and the Soviet Union. Once, they aspired to nationhood of their own, and hoped to attain it at the peace conference after the First World War, when the colonial powers were redrawing the map of the Middle East. But the dream vanished with the discovery of oil on Kurdish lands, and the Kurdish area of Iraq was incorporated into the British mandate. Since the end of the mandate, in 1932, no Iraqi government has successfully integrated the Kurds into the political system.

Irbil, a city of about a hundred thousand people, is the capital of the Kurdish Autonomous Region, an area of three provinces in northeast Iraq where Kurds predominate. Its modern multistoried public buildings, placed on carefully tended lawns, seem centuries away from the dark alleys of the souk. Higher and a bit cooler than Baghdad, Irbil exhibits more energy at midday, and, from the look of the men on the street, there is no mistaking that the city is Kurdish. Nearly all wear the traditional Kurdish costume of baggy pants, short jacket, cummerbund, and sandals. Around their heads they wrap a scarf into a loose turban, which they like to wear at a rakish tilt. Many of them display a curved ceremonial dagger in their belts, and some carry more serious-looking weapons over their shoulders. Kurds are known as the toughest fighters in the Middle East, and the people in Irbil actually seem exhilarated at being on the edge of a war zone.

The Kurdish Autonomous Region, which was formally established in 1974, is the product of a commitment made by the Iraqi government in 1970. Anxious to put an end to a succession of Kurdish revolts but determined to maintain the territorial integrity of the state, the government offered the Kurds official recognition of their unique nationality, the use of Kurdish as an official language, the appointment of Kurds to key posts in national government, and the exercise by Kurds of a range of powers—particularly over education at the local level. However, the agreement fell apart before it could be fully implemented, and hard-line Kurds, with Iran's support, conducted a rebellion, which lasted from mid-1974 to mid-1975. With the collapse of the rebellion, some of the rebel forces withdrew into Iran, where they lived quietly until Khomeini rearmed them in 1979 and 1980, then turned them loose to wage guerrilla warfare on the Iran-Iraq border. In recent months Iranian units joined the rebels, and the fighting intensified. In response, Iraq's military command leveled some Kurdish villages to prevent their use by guerrillas. Though these tactics have generated anger within the Kurdish community, the forces loyal to Baghdad have retained the upper hand and there are even signs that the rebellion is waning.

In Irbil, I visited Sirwan Abd Allah Jaf, the chairman of the executive council for the area, in one of the city's many new buildings. Not surprisingly, he assured me that Iraqi Kurds overwhelmingly support the autonomy system. With representation at both the local and the national level, he said, Kurds actually have more rights than other Iraqis, and he characterized the rebels as agents of Persian imperialism. "There are very few of them," he said, "and they are pursued like criminals." Indeed, Irbil and the region around it, though heavily patrolled by armed forces in jeeps, showed no signs of being besieged. I saw none of the machine-gun units or tanks that are pervasive in, for example, Beirut. Most of the pursuing forces are themselves Kurds, committed to a unified Iraq, Jaf said, and they fight in Kurdish units, wearing Kurdish insignias on uniforms with baggy pants.

Not long ago, many observers believed that Iraq's internal divisions were too profound to permit the forging of a unified nation. Some believe it still. But for nearly two decades Iraq has enjoyed stable rule, with what is apparently widespread popular consent. The system is a one-party regime, of which the dominant figure is Saddam Hussein, who has been president since 1979. Saddam chairs the highest governing institution, the nine-member Revolutionary Command Council, which derives its authority from the Baath Party, of which Saddam is secretary-general. Together, Saddam and the R.C.C. make policy for a Council of Ministers, which is responsible for running the machinery of state. In 1980, an effort to broaden popular participation, the government established a two-hundred-and-fifty-member National Assembly, which was elected by universal suffrage and given limited powers over legislation. However, representatives of the landowning and mercantile classes, which dominated Iraq's previous parliaments, were proscribed from running. In the current National Assembly, three-quarters of the members are Baathists, and all have swore allegiance to Party principles; it is therefore, hardly a forum for dissent. By any definition acceptable in the West, Iraq is not a democracy—for one thing, the press is tightly controlled—yet neither does it seem to be governed in defiance of the popular will. In fact, contrary to the historical odds, the Baath has been remarkably successful, having not only built cohesion among the diverse subcultures into which Iraqis are grouped but also rallied the nation to fight a long, bitter, and bloody war.

Iraqis, when justifying their politics to Westerners, note that for seven hundred years they did not have a government of their own, but that is something of an understatement. For much of those seven hundred years, there was not even an identifiable country named Iraq. Islam was the principal object of popular allegiance, the concept of nationhood had been forgotten. Nationalist ideology, imported from Europe, did not appear among the Arabs until the twentieth century, moving from Beirut eastward through Damascus and reaching Baghdad on the eve of the First World War. From that war, more or less at the whim of the peacemakers, there emerged an Iraqi state, which Britain took, over angry Arab protest, as a mandate. By 1920, the Iraqis—Sunni and Shiite, Kurd and Arab together—had risen up against British rule. A year later, to mollify demands for more local power, the British crowned as King of Iraq the Hashemite prince Faisal, whose family had led an Arab revolt against the Turks during the war, and whose brother Abdullah they had already placed on the throne of Jordan. Faisal, an undoubted nationalist, was personally esteemed, but the British never let him forget that the monarchy was dependent on them. A parliament was established that was heavily weighted on behalf of their interests; it never developed into a major supporter of Iraqi nationalism. Without commitment to economic or social progress, the British did little to relieve the poverty of Iraqi life. The Arab Sunnis, who dominated the administration and the Army, had some stake in the monarchy, but the Kurds were indifferent to it and the Shiites worked to replace it with a theocracy. In this atmosphere, popular animosity to the mandate intensified, and allegiance to the Hashemite monarchy never took root.

By the end of the 1920s, an army officer named Nuri al-Said had become King Faisal's closest associate and the country's strongest political figure. In 1932, under a treaty that Nuri negotiated with Britain, Iraq was declared a sovereign state, but in fact the treaty simply exchanged the formal mandate for an indirect dependency. Despite the departure of most of the occupying forces, few Iraqis liked the arrangement, which seemed to link the monarchy more closely than ever to Britain. In 1935, the country had its first tribal revolt, and in 1936 it had its first military coup. In 1941, a military clique under Rashid Ali, a former prime minister, took over the government, and turned to the Nazis for support of its nationalist aspirations. In order to crush this coup, the British returned in strength to Iraq and, during the four years of their second occupation, restored the monarchy's dominance. King Faisal I was now dead and the throne was under the control of the ambitious Crown Prince Abd al-Ilah, a regent for young Faisal II, the old king's grandson. The chief minister of this government was Nuri al-Said, who proceeded to hang or imprison the leaders of the coup—presumably at Britain's behest—and thereby set off a prolonged vendetta between the monarchy and the armed forces.

The decade after the Second World War is remembered in Iraq for the rise of the Communist Party, a succession of riots and strikes, and the humiliating defeat of the Arab armies in Palestine. From Cairo, the revolutionary leader Gamal Abdel Nasser was stirring up nationalist sentiments, and Nuri's toleration of corruption, including the rigging of elections, accelerated the erosion of the political fabric. In 1955, Nuri made what may have been a fatal error in subscribing, at the urging of Britain and the United States, to the anti-Soviet alliance known as the Baghdad Pact, two of whose members were Turkey and Iran. That Iraq should be serving the ends of Britain, Turkey, and Iran, its longtime enemies, was inconceivable to the nationalists. By now, talk of reform had faded, and the prospect of revolution appeared on the horizon. In 1956, Nasser took on heroic dimensions for many Arabs after Egypt was attacked in the Sinai by Britain, France, and Israel, and emerged, thanks to help from President Eisenhower, with its territory intact. Nasser's triumph was a clear threat to the conservative Iraqi monarchy, and when Nasser proclaimed Egypt's unification with Syria in February of 1958, Nuri countered by announcing Iraq's federation with Jordan, where Faisal II's cousin, King Hussein, sat on the throne. To Iraqis, the federation looked like a desperate conspiracy of two pro-Western kings to defend themselves against the popular forces of Arab nationalism. On July 14, the Iraqi Army seized the royal palace in Baghdad and executed the royal family, including Faisal II and Crown Prince Abd al-Ilah. The following day, Nuri was discovered in disguise on a Baghdad street and was gunned down on the spot. A day later, his body was disinterred by an angry mob and dragged through the streets.

The military commanders who directed the coup quickly fell out over the issue of whether to join the Egypt-

Syria union. An army general named Abd al-Karim Qasim, unenthusiastic about being subordinate to Nasser, opposed the idea, and within a few months he had maneuvered his rivals out of power. For this he became the object of Nasser's wrath, which further alienated him from the national mainstream. Qasim knew he needed help, and, without a political program of his own, he turned to the Communists, the country's most highly organized political force. When an army garrison at Mosul rose up in protest, Qasim put it down in bloody fashion with the air force, assisted by communist irregulars. A week later, Qasim signed an economic agreement with the Soviet Union, and a week after that he withdrew Iraq from the Baghdad Pact. These moves stirred the Baath, then an obscure underground party, to action, and on October 7, 1959, a Baathi assassination team, which included Saddam Hussein, ambushed and wounded Qasim on Rashid Street. Though Saddam himself escaped into exile, seventy-eight Baathists were put on trial and imprisoned. It was the first time the Baath had seriously commanded the nation's attention.

It was incomprehensible to me that the Baath, virtually unknown to Iraqis in 1959, would be strong enough to bid for power four years later and—what was even more astonishing—win total control of the government before the decade was out. I asked Tariq Aziz, Iraq's foreign minister, to explain it to me. Aziz has been a Baathist since his student days, in the 1950s. When he was Minister of Information, he was wounded in Baghdad, in April of

1980, by a grenade thrown by a Khomeini supporter—an attack in which several students were killed. Aziz likes to talk about the early days, and, as a former English teacher, he does so with great facility.

"At the time of the 1958 revolution, it is true, the people did not know or care very much about the Baath," Aziz said. "But, when it appeared that the Qasim government was being manipulated by he Communists, people began to worry. The Communists were taking over a revolution they had not made. In contrast to the Chinese Communists, who were always Chinese, the Arab Communists were Soviet, and the Iraqi people didn't like that. Mao made Communism a Chinese phenomenon, but most of the Arab Communist leadership was from minorities—mainly Jews at the start, not only here but in Syria, Lebanon, and Egypt. Then, in the fifties, when the Jews left Iraq, the Communist leadership was Christian and Armenian. The Communists were well organized and knew how to seize opportunities; but they were isolated from the traditions of the people, and over the years their alien character did not change. They were against Arab nationalism. The problem for progressives after the 1958 revolution was that because they did not want to bring back the old regime they said nothing. The nation faced a similar dilemma. If they sided with the reactionaries, they would lose the support of the people, but if they did nothing they would lose out to the Communists. Qasim was not a Communist—he was a patriotic military adventurer with great personal ambition. He found that in trying to use the

Communists he was overwhelmed by them. The only party able to contain the Communists was the Baath. It was small, but it, too, was well organized. It was bold and could not be intimidated. It appealed to the patriotism of the nationalists and to the social goals of the progressives. Old ladies called themselves Baathists, because the Party was pro-revolution and anti-Communist. Gradually, the Baath came to be seen as the savior of the nation—even by those who had little involvement in politics."

Through 1961 and 1962, the Baath, whose strength had been in schools and universities, prepared itself for action by infiltrating key units of the armed forces. It also recruited and trained a secret civilian militia. In February 1963, the Party struck, first assassinating the chief of the air force, then attacking the main radio station, the Ministry of Defense, and a series of military installations. The Communists fought back bravely, and hundreds were mowed down in the streets by tank fire. On the second day of the coup, Qasim was captured at the Ministry of Defense and executed, leaving the Baath in power.

In a reign of terror during the ensuing months, the new government sought out and killed dozens of Communists, as well as other opponents of the coup. Meanwhile, far from seeking reconciliation with the Kurds, the Baathists waged war against them. And, like Qasim, they failed to reach an accommodation with Nasser. It was not long before the Baathi leaders, divided into radicals and moderates, were quarreling among themselves, and in November the government collapsed, to be replaced by a military regime headed by General Abd al-Salam Arif—a regime not totally unlike the one that the Baath had overthrown.

"To understand why so much blood flowed in those days, you have to remember that Iraq's history is not one in which political dissent has been allowed," Aziz told me. "From the beginning, the ideas of the Baath were democratic. We wanted to reach our goals through democracy, but under the monarchy there was no democratic means of doing it. Revolution was our only choice. Nuri Said did not tolerate opposition. I was a student in his days, and we had to smuggle in books to read. I'm not talking about *Das Kapital* but about Victor Hugo, Dostoyevski, Rousseau, Voltaire—the kind of liberal books that are in a home library in New York or Paris. Nuri Said was a product of Ottoman times. He set the tone by torturing and executing many Baathists—in fact, almost anyone who opposed him. Under Qasim, the Communists also used killing and torture, and we had to retaliate. It was not our policy to use force, but we had no other means of dealing with them. Our weakness in 1963 was that we were inexperienced, and incapable of running a government. Remember that most of our Party members were very young men. Then we were succeeded by the Arif regime, which was rightist, militarist, and nationalist, pan-Arab—and not much stronger than we had been. It was also reactionary in the South American sense, meaning corrupt. We went underground to rebuild our support, but justifiably, Iraqis remained skeptical of us. We had to prove that we had absorbed our previous experience and matured—that we would not make the same mistakes if we got back into power. We replaced our old leadership, and when we struck again, in 1968, we were ready to govern."

After its fall in 1963, the Baath passed from radical to more moderate hands, dominated by a faction composed of blood kin from the province city of Tikrit. Saddam Hussein, who had returned from exile during the Party's term in office, was a key member of this faction. His power grew and with it the prominence of Tikrit in the Baath's upper echelons—particularly within the security apparatus. Arab family names often reveal a person's hometown, and prudence finally caused the Tikrit crowd to drop the designation. Thus, Saddam Hussein al-Tikriti became simply Saddam Hussein, leaving Western journalists unsure whether to call him by the regal Saddam or by the not quite correct Mr. Hussein.

By 1968, the Baath, though still a secret party of no more than five thousand members, had regained much of its former influence within the armed forces, whereas, after the disgrace of the Arab defeat by Israel in the Six Day War, the Arif regime—now headed by Abd al-Salam's brother, Abd al-Rahman—seemed to have lost its moorings. On July 17, 1968, supported by dissident military units, the Baath conducted a coup so well planned that the Arif government folded without the firing of a shot. Abd al-Rahman Arif was permitted to go peacefully into exile, and the Baath was once again in power. In the two years following the coup, the Party consolidated its position by the trial and execution of nearly a hundred Iraqis, of whom some were Communists, right-wingers, and some Jews accused of spying for the Israelis. Only when the Baath no longer felt menaced did the level of ruthlessness decline.

"The democratic tendencies among us remain alive," Aziz said, a bit defensively. "But, once in power, we had a social and political vision to protect, and we did what was necessary. After the revolution of 1968, we proposed to establish a national front, and we opened a dialogue with the Communists, the Nasserites, the Kurds, and others. We were willing to let the Communists reorganize their party and have a newspaper, but they also wanted power inside the army. They wanted a secret organization, which would have permitted them to plot another coup d'état. We would not allow this, and when they insisted we cracked down on them. And the Communists are not the only threat to the revolution. We are equally ready to punish the fundamentalist Shiites linked to Iran, because they are not patriots. We will tolerate dissent but we will not tolerate someone who cries, 'Down with the government!' For example, we will not punish a professor who criticizes the Ministry of Higher Education. If someone doesn't like the way we are running the government and wants to discuss alternative ideas with us, we will listen. There is dissent of this sort within the Party and the press. Furthermore, I assure you that when the war ends we will not stick to the one-party system. We don't believe in it. But we did not then and we do not now tolerate conspiracies.

We will not tolerate Communist conspiracies, and we will not allow a penny to enter the country from abroad to help the Communists substitute their revolution for ours."

Within a few months of the Baathi takeover in 1968, Saddam Hussein emerged as the strongman of the regime. As the revolution matured, he reshaped the Party from an underground elite into a ruling instrument in which civilians predominated over the military and which solicited a wide membership to work for the regime within a pyramidal structure with its base at the neighborhood level. He concluded the autonomy agreement with the Kurds. He presided over the nationalization of the oil fields—the last remaining symbol of foreign power in Iraq, and the source of its future wealth. He went to Moscow and returned bearing a strategic alliance with the Soviet Union which brought arms without significant Communist influence. He negotiated an agreement with the Shah of Iran—trading, territorial claims for an Iranian promise to stop promoting Kurdish and Shiite opposition—which brought calm to the country's eastern frontier. He poured subsidies upon the Shiites, and presided over the development of a socialist economy and a welfare state, giving particular attention to the problem of literacy. (Iraq now has seven universities, with well over a hundred thousand students—triple the number of twenty years ago. Education is compulsory through elementary school; high-school education is free; and thanks to adult literacy courses, nearly every Iraqi can at least now read a newspaper.) He gave the government a reputation for integrity beyond anything Iraq had known before—indeed, beyond anything known in the Arab world—and to demonstrate his seriousness he did not hesitate to have ministers and other high officials executed for corruption. At the same time, he strengthened his hold over the country by placing members of his family in the most sensitive positions of power. By 1979, when he was named president, the title merely confirmed the very wide powers he already held.

As Saddam's rule' solidified, the government began actively promoting—though it piously denies any such intent—a cult of personality around him. Saddam Hussein's picture appears in the press every day. He is on television not just for official pronouncements but to urge children to study hard and brush their teeth. Loyalty to Saddam is taught in the schools, and his role in the attempted assassination of Abd al-Karim Qasim in 1959 has been transformed into legend. His style of dress, his manner of speech, his mustache are imitated by nearly every Party member; and his face appears on the dial of the wristwatch that many of them wear. When he began to slim down recently, after acquiring a middle-age belly, half of Iraq went on a diet. He is referred to as "His Excellency" or "Out great President Saddam Hussein"—designations routinely followed by "May God keep him." The new airport, a new art center, and a new working-class district of Baghdad have been named for him. And, as every visitor to Iraq has noted, his portrait is ubiquitous—on display not just in public buildings but in cafés, in private homes, along roads, in hotel lobbies, in the town square of even the remotest village.

"I know you won't believe me whet I say that nearly all this is spontaneous," Tariq Aziz said. (In fact, I did not.) "You Americans have a different experience. We don't understand much about *you,* so we shrug our shoulders and say, 'That's how they live.' Well, since Hammurabi, we had lived without ever choosing our own head of state, so we have a different feeling about leadership. In this part of the world, we have an instinctive love for our leader, if he really is a leader. The people in Egypt loved Nasser. They made poetry and sang for him. Iraqis loved and respected King Faisal I—though never Nuri Said. They loved Qasim for a while. Then they found Saddam Hussein, the symbol of their aspirations, who really cares for them. He is strong. He is an Iraqi, like us. He raised himself from poverty, and he leads the first government since the Abbasid era to do something for the people. He is also a romantic figure. There is something chivalrous about him, which pleases both men and women. We can control what is hung in front of a government building, it is true, but we could never order parents to hang a photograph of Saddam Hussein in a child's bedroom. And yet it happens. Of course, the mass media make a contribution to Saddam's popularity, but they have not created him. The Iraqi people have contributed ten times as much to creating him. Saddam Hussein is in their hearts."

CHRISTOPHER KREMMER

The Carpet Wars

ONE OF THE WORLD'S FIRST great cities grew up on a marshy stretch of the Euphrates River on the western side of the Mesopotamian plain, about a hundred kilometers south of modern Baghdad. Its inhabitants called it Bab-Ilu, meaning "of the gods." The Hebrews called it Babel. We call it Babylon.

> CHRISTOPHER KREMMER
> *In* The Carpet Wars, *award-winning journalist Christopher Kremmer chronicles his ten-year odyssey along the ancient carpet routes of the Middle East. In this piece from 2002 we catch up with him in Baghdad.*

Here, in the fertile lands between the Tigris and Euphrates, tradition tells us the Garden of Eden was located. The Book of Genesis relates that it was Nimrod the Hunter, a descendant of Noah, who began construction of the city in the aftermath of the Great Flood, which submerged all the lands between the two rivers and beached the Ark on the side of Mount Ararat, eight hundred kilometers to the north. After the flood the Mesopotamians rebuilt.

"They had brick for stone, and they had asphalt for mortar," the Bible says, referring to the Babylonians' use of natural deposits of asphalt which bubbled to the surface as oil and, mixed with sand and gravel, congealed in the hot sun. They used it to build highways as well, but the bitumen road on which I now sped south was of more recent vintage. It slid past willow groves, police checkpoints, and low-slung whitewashed buildings. Beside it boys thrashed donkeys and powerline towers loomed over the salt marshes like giant steel centurions. There was no sign marking the 33rd parallel of latitude, but when we came to a mobile surface-to-air missile-launcher parked by the road I guessed we were near it. The launcher was raised at a sharp angle, ready to fire at American and British warplanes which flew scores of sorties every day, patrolling the Southern No-Fly Zone almost directly overhead.

In August 1992 President Bush, acting without the approval of the United Nations Security Council, banned Iraqi aircraft flying south of the 33rd parallel or north of the 36th and ordered his air force to patrol the "air exclusion zone." The idea was to protect Shiite Muslims in the south and Kurds in the north from Saddam's predations. In the days after Operation Desert Fox the cat-and-mouse game involving American and British pilots and Iraqi air defenses had intensified. Iraqi gunners could expect instant national celebrity if they brought a plane down. It was even dangerous to stand close to mobile launchers like the one we had seen, because laser-guided missiles fired by American and British pilots were constantly destroying them. But unlike the Gulf War, the Shiites and Kurds had not revolted during "Desert Fox." They still blamed Bush for encouraging them to revolt in 1991, only to stand by and watch as Saddam's Republican Guard slaughtered tens, possibly hundreds, of thousands of people. All too late, Bush realized that if Saddam was overthrown, Iran might exploit the disorder to seize Shiite-majority southern Iraq.

The Kurds—tough, Sunni Muslim mountain-dwellers whose language was similar to Persian—also had bitter memories of the Bush Administration. Early in his presidency on March 16, 1988, Iraqi Air Force planes bombarded the Kurdish-majority city of Halabja with mustard gas and nerve agents. The gas, which witnesses said smelt like burnt onions, killed an estimated five thousand people, mainly civilians, some of whom died laughing and dancing in the hysterical spasms induced by the chemical weapons.

Apart from Iran, Iraq is the only country with a Shiite Muslim majority. Two-thirds of Iraqis are Shiites, half the population of Baghdad likewise, and the sect's holiest places, such as Kerbala, where the Prophet's grandson Hussain is buried, are in Iraq. But whereas Iranian Muslims are Persians, Iraq's leaders see their land as an Arab country and throughout history have doubted the loyalty of Iraqi Shiites. This ancient mistrust made a democratic Iraq almost impossible to envisage. In a speech to his troops departing for the Iran frontline, Saddam reminded them of certain historical "facts," claiming that the Shiites had contributed to the conquest of Babylon by Persia's Cyrus the Great in the sixth century B.C., more than eleven hundred years before Islam was established. "They have co-operated with the Jews to destroy Babylon and co-operated with them to harm Iraq and the Arab nation," he said.

Almost two thousand years before Christ, the first great city of Babylon began rising beside the Euphrates. As well as being an important military and administrative center, it became a wellspring of religious and artistic inquiry, and it was here that astrology was invented. In 1760 B.C. the statesman Hamurabi developed and codified one of the world's first legal systems. Babylon was also one of the first major weaving centers.

"All the classical world knew and admired Babylonian carpets," wrote Arthur Urbane Dilley, although there is some debate as to whether Babylonian weavings were carpets or tapestries. Whatever they were, Pliny praised them in his *Natural History*, Nero bought them for use as table covers, and the Hebrews used them as tabernacle embellishments, as recorded in the Old Testament.

The city's fortunes waxed and waned, but in 605 B.C. the great warrior-king Nebuchadnezzar II began massive public works to revive its former glory, extending the city across to the west bank of the Euphrates and constructing the great stone terraces known as the Hanging Gardens of Babylon. The Babylonian historian and priest Berosus, writing in the third century B.C., described how Nebuchadnezzar had "built lofty stone terraces, made a vista as if of mountains, and planted all sorts of trees" because his wife Amytis was pining for the mountains of her native Media. Orchards, grapevines, and fig and olive trees graced the city, whose grandeur was capped by the famous Ziggurat of Etemenaki, more commonly known as the Tower of Babel, which rose almost ninety meters above the plain. Rebuilding the fortifications, palaces, and canals of the world's largest city, covering an area of about a thousand hectares, required a vast labor force which was provided when Nebuchadnezzar sacked Jerusalem and shipped his Jewish captives to Babylon, where they would remain for almost fifty years until freed by Cyrus the Great in 538 B.C. The Persians appropriated the city's arts, including carpet weaving. Alexander the Great intended making Babylon his capital, but [he was] weakened by his long expedition to Afghanistan and India, [and] his return was marked by tragedy when he died there in 323 B.C., aged thirty-three. . .

The gates of the great city stood before us now, conveniently situated across a car park. It was over a decade since I had beheld the majesty of the famed Ishtar Gate, named in honor of the Babylonian goddess of fertility, love, and war. Clad in glazed tiles of ultramarine, its wondrous procession of bulls and fanciful creatures guarded the city and its presiding deity, Marduk. It was an amazing sight, especially given that I had never been to Iraq. The entire Ishtar Gate stands in the Pergamon Museum in Berlin.

In June 1887 a German archaeologist, Robert Koldewey, visited Babylon and "saw a number of fragments of enameled brick reliefs, of which I took several with me to

Berlin." Twelve years later Koldewey returned with a well-funded expedition. Over the next thirteen years, he would excavate the city's major features including its main ceremonial entrance, the Ishtar Gate; its principal temple, the Esagila, dedicated to Marduk; and the great processional way, trodden by such giants as kings Nebuchadnezzar and Darius, and Alexander. The twelve-meter-high Ishtar Gate and processional way which linked it to the temple were decorated with colorful glazed ceramic tiles featuring lions, winged bulls, and the horned, fork-tongued walking serpents called *sirrush*, which boasted the front legs of a cheetah and the hind legs of a raptorial bird with powerful claws and great horny scales.

Herodotus claimed the walls of Babylon were fifty-six miles long, eighty feet thick, and over three hundred feet high. Although the city had never been lost, it was completely buried by centuries of Mesopotamian mud. With war clouds gathering in Europe, and Iraq a possible battlefield, Koldewey found a convenient excuse to remove a huge section of the ruins, including the entire Ishtar Gate, to Berlin.

"We were cramped for space," he later wrote of the sprawling site, "and could not spread out the pieces."

So moribund was Iraq after hundreds of years under Ottoman rule that its treasures were fair game for bespectacled European looters. Iraq has repeatedly demanded that museums in Britain and Germany return these important artifacts, but to no avail. In 2001, Britain signed the 1972 UNESCO convention on cultural property, but Germany remained outside it.

In place of the Ishtar Gate built for King Nebuchadnezzar II's city over two thousand years before stood a shoddy replica guarded by a gnarled, stubbly old man, who looked as if he'd been there since the Germans stole the original gate. The replica's colors were garish, the *sirrush* unbalanced and unglazed. Marduk had lost his protectors. Apart from Salar, the gatekeeper, and me, there was not another living soul in the place.

Starting our walk up the Street of Processions, we passed the new Ishtar Gate and headed uphill to the main palace. Our arrival was a melancholy affair. The reconstructed edifice, with its crenelated towers, was somehow flimsy, like something you might expect to see on a Hollywood movie lot. The walls of the palace rose some twenty meters high, most of it a cheap restoration built on the original shoulder-high foundations. Even here, Saddam's cult was inescapable. Every new brick laid during the Iran-Iraq War was stamped with the words: "Built in the era of the victorious Saddam Hussein, the great defender of Iraq and its glory." Saddam often compared himself to Nebuchadnezzar, especially in the late king's antipathy toward the Persians, and at Babylon a billboard depicted the two men and posters proclaimed: "From Nebuchadnezzar to Saddam Hussein, Babylon invokes its glories on the path of jihad and glorious development." But both the Hanging Gardens and the Tower of Babel had defied the efforts of archaeologists to positively identify them, despite Saddam's offer of a million-dollar prize to anyone who could restore life to the gardens.

After Alexander's death, the city had fallen into decay, local villagers carrying off the bricks to build themselves new homes. On the walls of the old city, large animal reliefs were visible, but the Lion of Babylon—carved from a single block of basalt, on which Ishtar rode—had been locked away. Near the main palace stood the artificial mound that some scholars believe is the ruin of the Tower of Babel. The original tower, as recorded in the Old Testament and recreated by the sixteenth-century Flemish artist Pieter Bruegel the Elder, was a seven-story ziggurat, with a sloping ramp spiralling around it to the top. The marvellous structure was a credit to human organization and endeavor, but God didn't like it.

> *And the Lord said, "indeed the people are one and they all have one language . . . now nothing that they propose to do will be withheld from them. . . . Come, let us go down and there confuse their language, that they may not understand one another's speech." So the Lord scattered them abroad from there over the face of all the earth, and they ceased front building the city.*

From Gilgamesh—hero of the Sumerian epic who sought immortality in vain—to Alexander, the curse of Babylon was reserved for the arrogant. Even Berlin was destroyed, but the Ishtar Gate survived.

On the Mediterranean island of Patmos you can enter the cave where John the Apostle sweated out the prophecy that became the Book of Revelation. John saw the

Euphrates dry up, and unclean spirits leaping like frogs from the mouths of dragons, the beast, and the false prophet all gathered at the place called Armageddon, and Babylon drank from the cup of God's wrath, and every island fell away, and the mountains were not found. Carried by an angel to a wilderness, John met a woman sitting on a scarlet beast, the Great Harlot with whom all the kings of the earth had fornicated, and on whose forehead was written:

MYSTERY,
BABYLON THE GREAT,
THE MOTHER OF HARLOTS AND OF THE
ABOMINATIONS OF THE EARTH

A golden hour settled on the plain near sunset and the date palm groves seemed to sigh as we left Babylon. Not far from the old city's gates, we turned off the road and, at my request, made our way into a village called Qaddassiya to conduct a random sample of local opinion. The rains having failed, the farmers of the area had moved their plots closer to the Euphrates, an old survival technique. As we entered the village, we encountered the local civil militia, gathered in a circle of chairs with Kalashnikovs resting on their knees. The wholly unexpected arrival of a foreigner brought them immediately to their feet, and blood-thickened voices filled the air.

"By our souls, and by our blood, we will sacrifice ourselves to Saddam Hussein," they cried, raising their guns.

The average age of Saddam's true believers must have

been sixty. They were farmers by day, and seemed to believe an American-led invasion was imminent.

"We are not going to move. You will not shake us. We love our president," they repeated, then confounded me by extending an invitation to dinner. But it had been a long day, and pleading a pressing commitment in the capital, we returned to Baghdad.

FREYA STARK

The Fellahin

IN EARLY SPRING, before the first buds show on the peach trees, a sort of luminous transparency envelops the distant city of Baghdad and its gardens. The pale minarets, the slowly swelling river, the desert itself with darker patches where fields of beetroot lie near the irrigation ditches, the russet lace-work of the willows so frail against the sky—all take on an ethereal quality, as of some faint angelic vision about to melt into its own heavenly atmosphere, some fugitive embrace of earth and sky which has left this print of loveliness behind it for the eyes of men. The blue domes melt into a heaven of their own color; the palm trees, bleached and pale after the winter, let the sun lie quiet as moonlight on their

FREYA STARK
In the mid 1920s, author and adventurer Freya Stark traveled from Persia to Yemen, mapping borders and discovering lost cities. Her 2000 book Baghdad Sketches, *from which this piece was taken, is an insightful glimpse into the history of Iraq.*

spiky polished crowns; and everywhere there is the voice of doves, sleepy and gentle, reminiscent of Solomon, and soft as the gray feathers which slip between palm and palm, or settle in crooning clouds on every cupola.

Nothing is loud, nothing is garish, except young blades of the autumn-sown corn that push up with the violence necessary to youth if it is to survive in the competitive world. Among the mongeese, under the columnar stems of the palms in the late afternoon, they catch the light and shine brilliant as halos not yet cut out into circles—so much more vivid than any mere terrestrial object has the right to be.

Before it has attained to this glory, however, and while yet the harmony of soft tones is unbroken, the spring has come, and all the lands that seemed so dead and dun around the city are filled with the bent figures of peasants, squatting over the ditches, squatting over the beetroots and lettuces, squatting over the low brushwood screens that protect their plants from the north wind. Only to the digging do they stand erect, having facilitated it by the invention of two men with a rope to stand in front of the digger and pull at his spade when he wants it out of the ground, a method which is said to enable three men to do the work of one in double the time: otherwise they are anchored to the earth to which they belong, and seem unable to separate themselves from it even to the extent of standing up straight on their two feet; they squat on their hams with a small sickle in their hand even to the cutting of their hay.

They are reserved people, not enterprising in friendliness like the peasants of France or Italy, and too busy with their immemorial toil to turn to look at a stranger as he passes. Their women, dressed in black like the Bedouin, with a small turquoise on one side of the nose and anklets to their feet, carry the produce to market on their heads; or, if there is much and it is far, they hang it on either side of a white donkey, of which the owner sits loosely on the tail. If you stop, however, and talk to them, they will wake from the dream of their labors, and answer in a pleasant enough manner, and give you news much like an English farm-hand on all points except the weather, which their piety does not allow them to prognosticate, even if the deluge plainly threatens; for they are still religious, having neither the self-reliant independence of the Bedouin nor the weak open-mindedness of the town.

One day E. asked me to go down to Rustum, which is the Government farm near the Diala, to see the peasants celebrate their annual banquet with a bonfire.

We were still in the last days of Ramadhan, so there was no question of dinner till after sunset, and as we reached the whitewashed mosque of Rustum village we found the crowd already gathered in early twilight, and great preparations going on in the matter of cookery in the women's part of the village huts. The men were squatting about in ample cloaks, speaking little and quietly as is the Muslim way on a holiday, the only animated part of the scene being the right-hand corner by the mosque, where the small boys were all gathered in charge of the Mulla, whose preoccupied efforts as he moved among them with short-sighted spectacles and green turban seemed quite insufficient to repress their natural spirits.

The mosque is a little model mosque, rather like a dissenters' chapel to look at, with rush matting laid all over the floor, very clean and neat and bare: here the feast was to be spread, with no feeling of incongruity among sensible people who do not take their holidays as things to be ashamed of in the sight of the Lord, and probably feel that he enjoys the picnics as much as they do. Anyway, there was something of the old hieratic pomp as the great copper trays were borne in shoulder high, with mountains of rice steaming like Fujiyamas unextinct and large cauldrons close at hand from which gravies and gobbets of mutton poured lusciously. Then there was a great sitting down, a matter of some arrangement considering the number of the invited and the amplitude of the garments, which tend to spread like a billowing sea around anyone inside them who is trying to sit on the floor: but eventually every tray was surrounded by its circle of devotees and the serious business of enjoyment began, in befitting silence, and with a rapidity which makes one realize why half the Arabs die of indigestion. In the twinkling of an eye those trays were empty, replaced by oranges, and by a general feeling of relaxation and expansion.

Leaving the management of affairs to the members of his staff, who were joint hosts in the feast, E. and I came out into the court of the mosque: here the colony of small boys, at last subdued to a proper solemnity, tucked into things in their turn under the paternal eye of the Persian

Mulla. Only the women, who are expected anyway to live on altruism in this world and content themselves with the sight of other people eating the works of their hands, had no official part; they hovered in the distance, watching as it were the steam of sacrifice, and no doubt wondering if their calculation of their husbands' appetites had left a margin over for their own suppers. E. felt sure it had, so that with a contented mind I was able to turn my attention to the preparing of the bonfire in the middle of the yard.

My education has been neglected in matters like arithmetic and correct behavior of many kinds, but I was properly brought up to worship fire. I remember as a small child being taken out to our Dartmoor "cleaves" after supper to watch the "swaling," and to dance with my sister round the burning furze bushes as they flared into the night. And I remember my father, in camps among the boulders on damp summer days on the moors, building up his fire with loving art, making a little hut of dryish boughs, and sods of dank earth outside, and a hole at the top for a draught, and then the precious piece of dry kindling for the innermost heart of the contrivance, to make it burn. And even in the house, where he used to lay the logs from our woods on a bed of ashes and arrange a semicircle of peats behind them to radiate the heat—even there one of the earliest remarks I remember when he came into the room was: "Damn those servants! Why can't they leave the fire alone?" which is surely fire worship, of a kind.

And other fires, terrible fires during the war, when ammunition dumps burnt through the night, flaring at minute intervals and lighting the hills of Gorizia, and the cruel hog's back of the Carso covered with dead, and the far Carnic Alps, with a devilish unforgettable beauty: or flaming villages during the sad retreat, burning three days and nights under the ram along the eastern sky. Who, having seen such things, can watch without dread and awe even the household fire?

The bonfire at Rustum, however, was made with a happy carelessness by the mere setting of a poplar tree, or the top of it, in the middle of the yard, and the producing of several matches: and into the light, out of surrounding night, leaped the faces of all the peasants, with their eyes, brilliant and soft as the night itself, fixed upon the flame.

They were varied in type, because sometimes the Bedouin when they are poor come and work upon the land, and their finer features and nobler walk still distinguish them among the rest: but mostly they were a nation of their own, with black eyebrows curved slightly like feathers, and faces more carefully modeled than the pudding-headed Sumerian of the town. "Will they dance for us?" I asked; and presently, after a little persuasion, the younger men lined up one behind the other and began to circle, chanting, round the flames.

The fire burned into the night, almost as high as the tree which gave it birth: it tossed sparks like a horse its mane, up into the unlimited darkness: and the peasants, chanting and jogging round, with a sideways jerk at every step, gradually forgot our chilling presence: one after another knives appeared, thick crooked blades held high above their heads: one of the effendis, a nice young man who evidently knew the secrets of the human mind, let off his pistol—which had an instant and delirious effect and turned the proceedings from a parade into a war dance.

The pace grew faster, the voices grew fierce, more branches were thrown to feed the flames, the short thick knives were silhouetted blackly, and more and more pistols went off, drawn evidently out of the civilized pockets of the young effendis and adding a frenzy with every explosion: if only it had been a real war dance with a village to loot at the end, looted it would have been—we were ready for anything. We began to understand the meaning of dancing, which fortunately one loses sight of in a ballroom.

This became more evident when, exhausted with War, two or three of the dancers began to fall into the softer steps of Love. A little boy in a yellow gown, with a red skullcap on his head, was evidently an expert: with clasped hands he wriggled his little body; his face sat motionless above it, old with an expression of unholy innocence, as if evil were as familiar as it was indifferent to him, since the very beginning of time: an embodiment, he seemed, of this primeval art, handed down on the Babylonian soil from the first ages of humankind, when movement was easier than speech.

But presently one of the dancers snatched a black *abba* from someone standing near by, and, turning himself into the most repulsive female ever imagined, advanced to the duct, while on the far side of the now smoldering fire the chorus beat on two trays and a drum and prepared to join in with interjections.

"Oh Ne'maka, there is no rose like you," sang the swain, contorting his body with a crack of his finger joints as he clasped his hands before him.

"I do not want you," says Ne'maka, leaping with unfeminine agility to the other side of the fire.

"I am ground like flour before you," sings the swain.

"There is no rose like you," the chorus repeats, and goes on repeating, beating on its drum.

"I will get you water from the river," sings the swain, now becoming so very caressing that E. evidently ponders whether it will not soon be time to take me away.

"I will make your bread," the swain is saying. "I will make your bed."

But Ne'maka, probably right, refuses to believe him, and with sudden leaps and crouching away from his attentions, repeats: "I do not want you" at every opportunity.

"I will make your food," says the swain, standing quite still and moving only his neck in the most remarkable manner.

"What is it you do want?" he sings at last, with the natural exasperation of practical man in face of woman's nebulous desires.

"Still I do not want you," says Ne'maka, and nothing could be clearer than that: and a good thing too, says my host, for heaven knows what the dance would have become had she relented.

The repulsive female now turned into someone called 'Aziza.

"Aziza comes swaying; dazzling in whiteness above them all," sings the swain.

"Like the ewe lamb of Halak, that runs after the shepherds."

She: "Him I saw by the river, beating his breast with stones."

He: "I will prepare you between my breasts a room that shines like gold."

She: "Alas, my mother's son, I am sorrowful; for your trouble is in vain."

He: "After the laughter, and the seizing of her waist, she became like an enemy."

She: "But one day he brandished his poplar pole, and all my branches grew limp."

He: "Oh, 'Aziza, a gazelle nurtured in my room and garden:

"Her locks are like creeping plants spread on the banks of a stream."

With the fire settling in its ashes and the drums still beating, E. and I left the feast, and found our way—out of how many thousand years?—to supper in the twentieth century.

SAÏD K. ABURISH

Cruel Ancestry

MUCH OF WHAT THE PRESS and biographers have written about Saddam [Hussein's] life is true. But it represents a one-sided story since it is limited to reports of his actions; no attempt is made to explain the background to his emergence on the world stage and to locate him in Arab and twentieth-century history. Judged absolutely and in comparison with those of his Arab contemporaries, his achievements are substantial, and some of them will outlive the current deafening noise surrounding his reputation. The possibility that he will occupy a place of honor in Arab history and condemnation elsewhere has to be understood in the context of the history of

SAÏD K. ABURISH *is a journalist who has worked as a consultant to the Iraqi government. Aburish occupies a singular role, condemning Saddam Hussein while simultaneously criticizing the West's aggressive role in Iraq. This piece is excerpted from a 2001 article.*

Iraq, its geopolitical position, its covetous neighbors and the major powers which believe Iraqi oil is so significant that they cannot leave the country alone.

Saddam's role and reputation must be weighed along with the unfulfilled desires of the Iraqi people, and their justified historical belief that they have been denied the right to realize the potential of their land and earn it a place among modern nations. In other words, Saddam as an individual may be unique, even demonic, but he is also a true son of Iraq. Even his use of violence to achieve his aims is not a strictly personal characteristic, but rather an unattractive trait of the Iraqi people reinforced by their history.

Thousands of years ago Mesopotamia ("the land between the rivers"), as it was known by the Greeks, was one of the great cradles of civilization. Its strategic importance on the overland route between Europe and Asia, combined with the agricultural potential of the rich fertile expanse between the Tigris and the Euphrates in an otherwise arid region, meant that it was constantly fought over. Ancient Mesopotamia is associated with dozens of kingdoms and empires: Sumerian, Akkadian, Babylonian, Hittite, Hurrian, Kassite, Elamite, Assyrian, and, in more recent centuries, Arab, Persian, and Ottoman. While some of these entities expanded, then contracted and often disappeared of their own accord, most of them replaced each other violently, through conquest or rebellion or a combination of both.

In the fourth century B.C., Alexander the Great captured Babylon and cut a swathe through the region on his eastward journey of conquest. In the eighth century A.D., by then already known as Iraq, it was conquered by Arab Muslims who established the Abbasid caliphate and built the legendary Baghdad. But even this flourishing empire, with its libraries, scientific achievements, and poetry, was anchored in violence: more than eighty of its ninety-two caliphs were murdered as a result of feuds over succession, corruption, or palace intrigues. In the thirteenth century, in an orgy of slaughter and looting, the Mongol hordes ransacked Baghdad and destroyed the great libraries, the cultural inheritance of the Abbasids. During the seventeenth and eighteenth centuries both the Persians and the Ottoman Turks tried to establish dominance over Iraq and turned it into a battleground; eventually the Turks incorporated the territory into the Ottoman Empire. From the late nineteenth century the British sought to control Iraq to safeguard their route to India. After the First World War and the defeat of the Turks, Britain occupied Iraq and briefly administered it as a mandate territory. What followed was a monarchy of Britain's creation.

The violence and cruelty which accompanied every change in the governance of the country throughout its history occasionally took novel forms which left an indelible imprint on the local population. Two examples stand out. Upon entering the city of Najjaf in 694 A.D., the Muslim conqueror Al Hajjaj Bin Yusuf Al Thaqafi described the Iraqis as people of "schism and hypocrisy" and declared, "I see heads ripe for cutting and verily I am the man to do it." When in 1258 Hulagu, the grandson of

Genghis Khan, laid siege to Baghdad, he bombarded the fortified inner city to rubble and ordered the breaking of the dykes on the Tigris, thus drowning most of the population. It therefore comes as no surprise that, on hearing of the killing in 1958 of the British-backed royal family, the Hashemite descendants of Muhammad, the Orientalist Freya Stark wrote, "Even the massacre of the prophet's family is no novelty on that soil."

Leaving human violence aside, the natural environment itself has been no kinder to Iraq. Floods, earthquakes, plague, famine, and the wretchedness of a land where the temperature can fluctuate by forty degrees centigrade within a single day have contributed to the emergence of an indigenous personality at war with nature and the rule of man. Every conqueror left people and aspects of their culture behind, and the depopulation of the original inhabitants through natural disasters, civil strife and war allowed the new arrivals to create a greater impression than would normally have been the case. The influence of the Mongols who remained after their conquest, for instance, was considerable because two-thirds of the original population had been massacred. By the twentieth century the country contained a rich ethnic and religious mix of Arabs, Kurds, Turkomans, Persians, Chaldeans, Yezedis, Sabaens, and Jews, along with smaller groups of Afghans, Azeris, and Hindis. Even in the 1920s, 44 percent of the members of the chamber of commerce were Jewish. In the words of the celebrated journalists John Bulloch and Harvey Morris, Iraq remains the least Arab of the Arab countries.

The turbulent history, harsh environment, and multi-stranded culture of Iraq have produced a complex and unique conglomerate which lacks the ingredients for creating a homogeneous country and a commitment to the idea of a national community. Modern Iraq is a fractured society in which numerous clusters, tribes, ethnic and religious groups pay genuine tribute to the idea of a nation state, but one which accords paramountcy to their particular tribal, ethnic, or religious background.

The schism between Sunni and Shiite Muslims typifies the problem. This religious split began in A.D. 680 over the nature of the prophet's succession, and grew under Persian and then Ottoman Turkish rule. The Persians promoted their Shiite co-religionists, while Sunni Turkey supported its own. Each group mistreated the others when in power and denied them their rights, and the cleavage eventually assumed a socio-economic nature—since Turkish supremacy lasted longer than Persian it gave the Sunnis an educational and wealth advantage over the Shiites which still remains. Today, most Sunni Muslims are Arab nationalists who want union or closer relations with the rest of the Arabs, while many Shiites work toward closer ties with Iran. Thus conflicts between narrow loyalty and the larger dream of nationhood are constant, and lie behind the incoherence and habitual disorder which racks the country.

Saddam Hussein is not the first, nor is he likely to be the last, dictator of Iraq. When such a neurotic individual superimposes himself on this arena of discord, we are confronted with a ruler suffering from a patterned defect. In Saddam's case there is a morbid, dangerous preoccupation with creating a whole out of the disparate parts. I call it a patterned defect because most Iraqis suffer from it. Given the opportunity, each of them would pursue Saddam's aim of creating a unified, strong Iraq in his own way.

However, despite the cultural mélange, the character of Iraq is basically Arab. This is because the Arabs, who ruled the country for six centuries, had a religion which produced a developed culture. Their predominance was reinforced by the movement into Iraq of tribes from the Arabian peninsula. The Arabness of Iraq has been part of the search for a unifying national identity. Saddam's commitment to meld what exists on the ground under the umbrella of Arab culture was tried by many leaders before him, though in a less deliberate and brutal manner. This is why there have been many occasions when being Arab was subordinated to being Iraqi, when the latter was considered to be more of a unifying umbrella, even under Saddam Hussein.

The arrival of the British during the First World War, and their subsequent occupation of the country, compounded the legacy of the Persians and Ottoman Turks. Discovering that imposing direct rule on Iraq was unaffordable, the British sided with the more educated minority Sunnis (then, as now, around 20 percent of the population) and used them to perpetuate the inequality that the Turks had created. (Former Iraqi cabinet member Abdel Karim Al Ozrie claims that the extensive Iraqi diplomatic service did not have one Shiite ambassador until 1956.) But those who laid the foundations of modern Iraq during the past two centuries also left a lasting impression on the land which went beyond building an unsound political structure. To this day Iraqi Arabic is replete with non-Arabic words, mostly Turkish and Persian but some introduced more recently. *Fasanjoon*, an Iranian dish, has been claimed by many Iraqis as their own. The word for "good" is not Arabic but the Turkish equivalent, *khosh*. Lack of good manners is described in a phrase which also recalls the days of Ottoman Turkey, *adab sis*. And even a whorehouse is a *kharakhanah*, for it was the Turks who introduced these establishments to Baghdad and other cities. The Iraqis use the English "glass" instead of its Arabic equivalents, *cass* or *kubaya*, and the upper classes say "countryside" instead of *rif*.

Nevertheless, despite being the offspring of its tortured historical search for identity, Iraq does have a distinct social and economic character. This came into being in the mid-nineteenth century, when the Turks introduced the *tanzimat* (the concept of organization through codifying the law) and tried to turn the country into a functioning territory within the Ottoman Empire. Contrary to the claims of Orientalists, which the press adopt too readily, the country as a geographical unit was always united by the two rivers and, except for a relatively brief period toward the end of Ottoman Turkish rule, authority under them was centered in Baghdad. The legend which claims that Iraq is a country stitched together by the

British from three *villayats* or provinces, Baghdad, Mosul, and Basra, is shallow. Turkey created these *villayats* by decentralizing from Baghdad for a brief time before the First World War. The historian Malik Mufti refutes the claim without hesitation by stating that "Iraq [as created by Britain] was not an entirely artificial concept."

What victorious Britain did produce after the First World War was an Iraqi government which controlled the same territory that Saddam Hussein governs today. It confirmed those borders in 1926, five years after it had established the Iraqi monarchy and imported an Arab king, Faisal I, to deputize for it while investing real authority in the British High Commissioner. It is true that the boundaries of modern Iraq were drawn in response to Western interests, in accordance first with the 1916 Sykes-Picot Agreement, which divided the Middle Eastern spoils of the First World War between Britain and France, and later in recognition of the British desire to control the city of Mosul and its oil. But the core of Iraq as a place with a people was already in existence under the Ottoman Empire and even earlier.

The British and the new monarchy worsened the historical problems which had always bedeviled the country. The imported king had never been to Iraq before the British appointed him. He belonged to the minority Sunni sect and, above all, he ruled without governing. Faisal himself accepted the paramountcy of the High Commissioner and admitted that he was no more than "an instrument of British policy;" the Orientalist Gertrude Bell, one of the people behind Faisal, wrote to her father on July 8, 1921, to complain about how tiring "making kings" was. The opinion of the majority Shiites was totally ignored. To support Faisal, the British took the easy way out and elevated to positions of power Sunnis who had served as officers under Turkey.

In 1920, just before the plans for imposing the monarchy were finalized, the Shiites rose up against the infidel British and their plans. Because most Iraqis wanted to be independent and free, the rebellion eventually spread to include those Sunnis outside the small, elite circle whom the British were promoting. Both Muslim sects turned against the *franji*, the European usurper, and the result was some two thousand British casualties including 453 dead. The strength of the uprising caused the British to resort to two elements of warfare which have been copied by Saddam in more recent times: they employed their air force against civilians and they used gas. The Christianity of the British, the lateness of their conquest, their lack of sensitivity to local conditions (which included dependence on a minority), and their willingness to resort to force and chemical warfare administered a shock to the country's social system from which it has never recovered. It was the British conquest of Iraq which set the stage for what is happening today.

Along with ignoring the Shiites the British allowed the promise to grant the Kurds independence, which had been included in the 1920 Treaty of Sèvres, to lapse. Iraq as represented by the Shiites, the Kurds and those Sunnis, mostly from the lower classes to which Saddam's tribe belonged, who sought independence—in total, nearly 70 percent of the population—was now resolutely anti-British. As a result the conquerors were forced into even heavier reliance on the Sunni aristocrats, who were allowed to control the government. There were also some Shiites tribal leaders who succumbed to the enticement of land grants, former officers in the Turkish Army who were made generals and ministers and were also given land, Jews, who got special protection, and the Assyrians and other minorities who were employed in the new administration.

Operating with a shackled king who proved more astute than they had anticipated and who lamented the absence of social cohesion in his country, the British later added to the explosive situation by supporting the tribes to undermine him and by creating a special force of Christian levies to use selectively to protect their interests and oil installations. They opened a direct line of communication with the leaders of the abandoned Kurds and used them intermittently to support and undermine the central government. In fact, they dealt directly with the small ethnic and religious segments of Iraq and the leadership of the Kurds and Shiites without deferring to the Sunni government that they had created—among other things, they stipulated that the Minister of Finance be a Jew.

Just as the long-term history of Iraq contained and nurtured violence, the British, following short-sighted policies similar to those employed by Iraq's ancient conquerors, contributed measurably to the ethnic, religious and social divisions which beset the country. Because the average Iraqi was beyond their reach, British policies precluded the creation of a democracy and included looking the other way while supporters of Britain, even some prime ministers, murdered and imprisoned popular politicians in the tradition of the centuries-old Iraqi reliance on violence to express political opinion. The Kurds, among others, resorted to the gun to try to attain their national aspirations, and the Shiites sought Iranian support to undermine the government.

That violence continues to be part and parcel of the Iraqi personality is no accident. The monarchical system, which governed Iraq until 1958 and which the 1921 Peace Conference in Cairo designed, was unsound and contained the seeds of its eventual destruction. The historian H. V. F. Winstone cites the words of Gertrude Bell, a participant in the Peace Conference, to demonstrate how little attention was paid to the long-term effects of what was being discussed and planned. Her recollections of a conversation among three of the conference delegates went like this:

> *First statesman*: The country will be badly governed.
> *Second statesman*: Why should it not be badly governed?
> *Third statesman*: It ought to be badly governed.

There is no reason to suppose that they did not have Iraq in mind.

Although King Faisal was put on the throne of a country which was expected to be badly governed, he still tried his utmost to improve the situation and undertook moves, including recognition of Shiite rights, to bridge the gap between his realm's diverse components. Against British resistance, he devoted a great deal of time and effort to creating a strong army to give his country pride and to serve as a nucleus for integrating its people. Interestingly, his attempts at enfranchising all segments of the population included encouraging the Tikritis, Saddam's poor and ignored relations, to enter the armed forces. King Faisal died in 1933 before he fully realized his dream and was succeeded by his incompetent and hot-headed son, Ghazi. Instead of using the army to unite the country, by placing it above politics, Ghazi made it another instrument of division. In 1936 the semiliterate Ghazi colluded with General Bakr Sidqi and staged a coup, which ushered in a whole age of coups. The Army became a faction, a participant in the endemic violence, and politicians tried to control it and manipulate its composition.

Saddam Hussein was born about the time of Ghazi's suspicious death in 1939. He was the product of a poor childhood which produced bitter experiences that he has never forgotten or overcome. In many ways he is very much like all the rulers of Iraq since King Faisal I, but for his highly individualistic utter lack of psychological or sociological restraints. Saddam too has tried to unify Iraq through a strong army and, inventively, the use of the country's diverse past.

THE PEOPLE

MICHAEL KELLY

Mob Town

BAGHDAD IS RICH in monuments to the dead of war. They are, excepting the Leader's many palaces, by far the most impressive pieces or architecture in the city. Of the three major shrines, the most benevolent is the Monument of Saddam's Qadissiya Martyrs. Here, on December 1 of every year, the official Government ceremony is held to commemorate what is known by decree as Martyrs' Day, which honors everyone killed one way or another in service to the Leader.

MICHAEL KELLY *has been an editor with* The New Yorker *and the* National Journal *and is currently editor-at-large with the* Atlantic Monthly. *This excerpt is from his 1996 report for* The New Yorker.

At a quarter to ten on the morning of Martyrs' Day 1991—an unsuitable morning, sunny and blue and unseasonably sweetly warm—a few hundred people were lined up in patient quietude before the heavy black steel security fence that guards the entrance. The fence is set on wheels in tracks, and opened and shut by electrical impulse. It was a professional crowd of mourners: soldiers, schoolchildren, government workers, and party hacks. Bureaucrats fussed around and through the crowd, herding everyone into just-so order. They were from the Ministry of Information and Culture, and they were known as minders. As a foreigner, I had a minder assigned just to me, and he hovered at my shoulder like a hummingbird, nervous and eager to please.

In the vast and cruel hierarchy of the Iraqi state minders are important enough to be disliked by their colleagues and charges, but not important enough to be respected or feared. The spies that matter, the sleek young louts of the Mukhabarat (the largest of the state's five intelligence agencies), have the power to torture and kill, and act like it. They wear sunglasses, black vinyl jackets and pleated Italian trousers, and swagger about Baghdad like Toonland gunsels. Minders wear the genteel-shabby suits of the clerking class. Formalized snitches, classroom monitors, they inspire only resentment and sneers behind their backs. They suffer from low self-esteem. In three trips to Iraq, I never learned their proper title. Everyone called them minders, and they even called themselves by this mildly deprecating term: "Hello. I am your minder today," or "If you are going to go to the market, you must remember to take a minder."

At 10 A.M., the two long center sections of the iron fence enclosing the grounds of the monument jerked apart with a grinding, clanking rumble, and, after a moment's hesitation, the crowd moved forward—slowly, silently—up a long gray granite walk to the monument's vertical center, a giant blue eggshell set in a field of white marble and split longitudinally in half. At the front of the procession were the guests of honor, two war widows and an orphan. The widows were suitably dressed in black, but the little girl wore a bright pink party frock, puffed up with layers of frilly slips underneath.

Behind them came several platoons of boys dressed as soldiers, in crisp fatigues of blue or tan cloth stamped with a camouflage pattern. They wore gold epaulets on their narrow shoulders, and pink and white scarves around their skinny necks. They were no more than ten or eleven years old, and they were members of al-Talaia (the Vanguard), the state organization for citizens between the ages of ten and fifteen. Political indoctrination in Iraq actually begins when children enter school at the age of five or six, but al-Talaia is the first political and paramilitary group to which one can belong. The young soldiers of al-Talaia learn to march, to follow orders, and to serve as junior agents of the state, spying and filing reports on their peers and, on occasion, their parents. The little troopers marched up the walk as a unit, with a childish semblance of military discipline, pumping their arms and swinging their legs in goose-stepping exuberance. Some carried bright paper parasols, which they twirled in ragged coordination. They chanted as they marched: "Long life to the Baath Party! Long life to Saddam Hussein!"

At the base of the great blue eggshells, the marchers merged with an honor guard already in place. There were half a dozen units, all in parade dress, gaudy and gleaming in the morning sun. The Republican Guards were the most glorious, decked out in uniforms as fine as Victoria's own fusiliers—red tunics with blue sashes and tall topees with gold chin straps below and gold tassels stirring in the breeze above. They played drums and horns and clarinets, ushering in the mourners with a tune of vaguely Sousa-ish nature. "It is a national song, very popular," my minder said. "It is called 'We Welcome the National War.' "

A couple of hundred feet of red carpet had been unrolled up the center of the approach to a pale little flame—almost invisible in the sunlight—in between the eggshells, and the assemblage gathered at the foot of the carpet. Everyone was orderly. The only people making any noise were the musicians of the Republican Guard and the boys of al-Talaia, who had taken up the traditional song on these occasions.

"With our blood, with out souls, we sacrifice for Saddam," they trilled in their pretty, light boy-voices.

The ceremony did not take long. First, six middle-aged men in suits from the Arab Baath Socialist Party walked up and laid a wreath in front of the small gas flame. Then four middle-aged men in suits from the Iraqi National Student Union laid down their wreath. Then five men and one woman from the Iraqi National Teachers Union.

And so on and on it went, all of a bleak, bleached sameness, each delegation trudging up the last few steps to the flame with a slow, funereal gait, laying down its wreath as the honor guard jigged, and trudging back the General Secretariat of Iraqi Economic Advisers, the Iraqi Geologists Union, the Iraqi Doctors Union, the Union of Employees of the Ministry of Foreign Affairs, the Iraqi Women's Federation, the Iraqi Friends of the Children Association, the General Federation of Arab Women, the Union of Employees of the Ministry of Information and Culture.

As each group approached, my minder read its name off the wreath and whispered it in my ear. Once, he got excited. "Here is a group coming up that has no name on its wreath," he said. The oddity of this caused him to fall prey to sudden false hope. "Maybe it is just citizens," he said. But then the breeze blew away a palm leaf that had been hiding a tag. "Oh," said the minder. "No. It is the Union of Employees of the Ministry of the Interior."

He seemed a little embarrassed, but the paucity of ordinary citizens was hardly his fault. Over the last quarter century, the Leader had killed off, one way or another, an astonishing number of the ordinary citizens of Iraq, and many of those left living in the winter of 1991 were too crippled or drunk or hungry to gin up much enthusiasm for the celebration of their condition.

A few days later, in a quiet, modestly rich neighborhood in the western part of Baghdad, a woman was talking. She was from an ancient, wealthy, learned family, and she ran one of its businesses, a small construction firm. She was middle-aged, unmarried, and she had a strong, ugly-handsome face, with a powerful nose and a large mouth full of big, slightly yellow teeth. Her hands were like a working-man's: stubby fingers stained with chemicals and nicotine, palms hard and horny with calluses. She used her hands with theatrical artistry to emphasize her points as she spoke, making daggers and pointers and cups as the need arose. She smoked one cigarette after another, puffing furiously along,

"It breaks my heart, I tell you, what I see in my country now. It is much worse than people going hungry, or losing their money. What we are seeing here is the moral disintegration of a society. Pimping, thieving, murder, prostitution—it is all going on all the time now. There is only 2 percent of the country left that is honest, and half of that 2 percent is sitting at home doing nothing. They are too afraid to go out. Everyone is afraid.

"Crime is everywhere. When you drive at night, you keep the windows rolled up and the doors locked. Theft insurance has doubled on homes, and insurance premiums on cars are up 300 percent. People won't stay out late; it's too dangerous. The biggest robbers are the police. Men come to your house in uniform and take you to the interrogation center for questioning, and when you come back six hours later, you find that they have stolen all the furniture. Bastards.

"The only currency worth anything anymore is five- and twenty-five-dinar notes. The rest are forgeries. At first, they said it was Iranians and Saudis doing the counterfeiting, but the truth is that the biggest printing press in the country is right in the basement of the Ministry of Defense, where Saddam's son-in-law was Minister. It is the counterfeiting that is making the big party officials and the Government men so rich. The way it works is they buy gold with the counterfeit money. People don't want to sell gold for dinars, of course, but when you are a man in power, you can oblige them to sell to you.

"A tube of toothpaste right now costs eighteen dinars. But you cannot even find any toothpaste in the shops. Do you know why? Because there is one merchant who has cornered the toothpaste market. He bought all there was to buy in Amman. And he has taken all that toothpaste and put it in warehouses, and he is sitting and waiting for the price to go up to twenty-five dinars and then he will bring it out to sell. It is this way all over. Warehouses full of goods tucked away. Fat cats getting fatter.

"There are so many people who are starving here, whole families slowly starving away. Of course, the people in the Government do not live the way we live. They can get whatever they want. These people are actually frightened that the sanctions will be lifted. They have made millions and they want to make millions more."

All that this woman said was true. The war that had liberated Kuwait City had also liberated Baghdad, freeing it to reach, you might say, its fullest expression of self. It had become the ideal mob town, the perfect capital of a gangster nation. The new millionaires, Baathist bosses, Government ministers, and their merchant friends, tooled around the city in Mercedes-Benzes the color of créme fraîche and swaggered through the casinos tossing stacks of new money on the baccarat tables.

The biggest man about town was Uday, Saddam's oldest son, whose new newspaper, *Babel*, had attracted great numbers of readers with its gossipy tone and its daring columns poking fun at low-level bureaucrats. Uday and his entourage were out most nights, dancing, drinking, whoring, gambling, and occasionally beating up passers-by.

Only the rich and the politically connected could afford to eat much. The Government doled out some food, but never enough, and the Western relief workers in Baghdad had come to realize, after their offers of assistance had been stymied time after time, that the Government wanted things exactly the way they were. The deaths of the poor turned national anger outward, toward the United States, and the hunger of the middle classes kept them too preoccupied to plot rebellion.

If you had money, though, the city was a treasure pot. You could buy a two-hundred-year-old carpet for $150, a one-hundred-year-old gold pocket watch for $50, a twenty-year-old virgin for $20. The streets were crowded with trucks loaded down with liquor and cigarettes from Amman. The lobbies of the big hotels were busy with formerly respectable young women sipping tea and pretending they were waiting for someone they knew, with United Nations officials staggering under the weight of their daily shopping sprees with sleek, sly Jordanian hustlers whispering in the ears of large men in too-tight suits who looked like aging mob muscle, but were in fact ministers of state.

There are many private clubs in Baghdad for the use of Government and high party officials: the Mansour Club, the Zowarak Club, the Hunting Club, the Alwiyah Club, the Al Khar Sporting Club (managed by Uday), the Saladin Club (for Quisling Kurds), the Assyrian Club, the Armenian Club. The evening of Martyrs' Day, a well-connected lawyer I had met by chance on a previous trip to Baghdad took me to the Alwiyah, next door to the Sheraton Ishtar Hotel in the center of town. The British built the Alwiyah in the 1920's, and although it has become somewhat run-down, it still looks very much like an English club—with three drinking rooms on the ground floor, a huge dining room, eight tennis courts, and three swimming pools. "It is very nice in the afternoon to sit on the lawn and drink Pimm's Cup," the lawyer said. In the evening, jacket and tie are required, and the crowd is mostly men; women are restricted to the dining room and the smallest of the bars.

We arrived about 9:30 P.M., late for the cocktail hour, but the biggest of the drinking rooms was still packed. The men sat in plush upholstered armchairs, grouped in fours and fives, around low tables, each crowded to the edges with bowls and plates of food (*lebenah*, bread and cheese, pickled beets, and carrots) and many bottles, mostly of Scotch (Johnny Walker, Haig & Haig, Pinch, Cutty Sark). The men leaned forward over their paunches and ate with their fingers, scooping up globs of hummus and baba gannouj, and gulping down tumblers of whisky. They talked in loud, drunken voices.

"They will drink like this until midnight perhaps, and then they will go out to nightclubs for more drinking or to stuff themselves with more food," said the lawyer, contempt in his voice. "Some will go to their prostitutes and mistresses," he said. He had been educated in England and wore fine tweed jackets and fawn-colored trousers and silk ascots, and smoked a briar pipe. He spent much of every year in London and New York, and saw himself as a cosmopolite.

Across the hall in the main saloon, an old-fashioned English men's bar, every stool was filled with men drinking. We drank with them for a short while, and afterward we went to a fancy restaurant, a place with damask tablecloths, a headwaiter in black tie, waiters in white dinner jackets, and everything soft and pretty in the candlelight. We dined on chauteaubriand, with pommes soufflés and baby green beans in a butler sauce, and drank a good Chianti Riserva, 1970, while on a gleaming black grand piano, a man played Cole Porter tunes.

Most of the drinking going on in Baghdad, and there was a savage amount of it every night, was on a less exalted level. One night I went to a little store a few blocks from the Sheraton, to pick up a bottle to take to a friend's house for dinner. As I walked in, the proprietor was counting the bottles in a shipment of Black Jack whisky, a vile concoction made in Lebanon and trucked in from Amman, He was in his thirties, I guessed, but looked older; he was tall and very skinny, and the planes of his face had been thinned down to gray hollows. Although it was a warm evening, he wore an old gray suit coat buttoned all the way up over a sweater, and a red and blue muffler wound around his throat. While we talked, he sat most of the time on a three-legged stool behind the counter; I gathered from the awkward movements he made when he was obliged to stand and fetch something that there was something wrong with his legs or hips. Gap-toothed, he spoke with a faint lisp, very softly, all the time smoking cigarettes and frequently coughing.

"No one buys anything except booze anymore," the proprietor said. Behind him were shelves containing a few food items and some bottled water, but 90 percent of the space was devoted to liquor. There were seven brands of arrack and all sorts of whisky, gin, vodka, Bulgarian red wine, and something called Kassatly Brut Pecher Mignon Vin, a Lebanese champagne made by mixing peach extract and alcohol.

"If you ask a person 'Do you want bread or whisky?' they will choose whisky," the proprietor said. "They all want to drink as much as they can, all the time—because they want to forget. Forget the war, the cause of the war, the war before this war, the man who makes us go to war, the people in the hospitals with no arms and no legs, the girls who cannot find husbands and the girls whose husbands are dead."

Outside the shop, a party was making its way to the Sheraton—a noisy parade of young men and cars careening up the street with drums and kazoos and whistles and high-yelping brass horns. It was a wedding, and there were many of them every night. Two wars back to back had postponed the unions of young Iraqis for a decade, and now the pent-up demand was giving way to an orgy of marrying. This procession consisted of seven or eight cars, mostly taxis, led by a Mercedes done up with ribbons, streamers, and blinking red, yellow and green lights. A taxi full of musicians followed the lead car, the three players leaning out the open windows, one blowing a horn, one sawing on a fiddle, and one banging a snare drum.

Baghdad weddings traditionally end with the bride and groom going into one of the hip hotels for a two- or three-day honeymoon. At the front door to the Sheraton, there were a half-dozen couples—each with their own little clanging, tootling street band—waiting to check in and to pose for photographs in front of the big statue of the goddess Ishtar in the center of the lobby. The brides were stacked up in a holding pattern like jetliners over a busy airport, each young woman stiffly moving forward a cautious bit at a time so as not to walk on the train of the one before. In front of Ishtar, a very young couple was standing for their photograph, the girl all ruffles and flourishes of white, with fishnet gloves that went up to her elbows.

Wandering later that night in the streets and in and out of bars, I fell in with a couple of very drunk men at the Palm Beach Disco Bar, a filthy dive on a honky-tonk stretch along the Tigris River. They were sitting at a table with one empty bottle of Scotch, two small empty bottles of arrack, and a half-filled pint bottle of Johnny Walker. The two of them—one very fat in a dirty yellow suit, the other very skinny in a gray ankle-length *dishdashah*—were smoking from an *agila*, the ornate brass water pipe that Westerners call a hubble-bubble.

The waiter brought a tumbler for me, and the fat man poured it half full of Scotch, and we drank and smoked the *agila*'s sweet tobacco, saturated with black honey and strawberry. The men were drinking to mourn the loss of the skinny one's job; he had been a brigadier general in the army, and had been cashiered after the war. "Very sad, very sad," he said, shaking his head in loopy, drunken wobbles. "Saddam bad, very bad."

He hauled his leg up onto the table and pretended to scrape crud off the sole of his shoe, wrinkling his nose in exaggerated disgust. "Saddam," he said, pointing to the imaginary scrapings on the tablecloth. We drank a toast to the Leader. The fat man blew his nose and held the handkerchief up. Another toast to Saddam. The skinny man spit in the ashtray. Another toast . . . and on it went until the whisky was gone.

Much later that night, driving wildly in the rain through back neighborhoods I knew nothing of, they took me to eat in a restaurant that, with its decor of tile, aluminum, and plastic and its menu of two dishes, perfectly represented the lowest common denominator of dining out in Arabia. "This is very good," said the fat man as we sat down. "Very special Iraqi food."

The platters in front of us held three boiled sheep's heads, steaming and covered by a grayish, whitish skin or membrane. You had to peel this off with your fingers to get to the next layer, which was a slab of pure fat. The fat was yellow and half an inch thick. I learned how to eat it from the fat man, who was sitting directly across from me, tearing off big hunks of the stuff, which slid greasy and wet in his hand. He opened his mouth wide, and shoveled the fat in as if he were stoking coal.

I couldn't make myself eat the fat, but moving it around on my plate, I found there was another layer underneath of a dark, oily meat. I pulled off a small piece and, with oversized gestures, to show that I was eating my share, held it up and put it in my mouth. It was spongy.

"Is good?" the fat man asked. "Is tongue, next to lips the best part."

After the tongue was gone, I ate some cheek, but not much. The fat man was hugely enjoying the meal. He had finished the fat and most of the easily accessible cheek, and was working on the finer points of the skull. Holding it up before him in both hands, propping his elbows on the table, he wrenched the lower jaw from the upper, stuck the jawbone in his mouth, and worked it like an ear of corn. He didn't miss a morsel, not even the little bits of gum between the shining teeth.

The party broke up around a quarter to two, when the skinny man fell asleep with his head on the table. The fat man drove me back to my hotel. As I was saying good-bye, he put his big right arm around my shoulders and pulled me close, while with his other hand he reached down and, to my surprise, gave a sudden, sharp squeeze to my penis. Whether his intention was to make a pass or merely to emphasize the point, I couldn't tell. Looking me deep in the eyes, he said: "Saddam bad. Bush good."

In the afternoons, in the same Sheraton Ishtar lobby where the brides promenaded at night, the new prostitutes sat in armchairs on the mezzanine nursing soft drinks or coffee. Many of them were war widows, I was told, and I thought how odd and unhappy it must be for them to find themselves selling themselves where they had honeymooned a few years earlier. A wealthy Jordanian hustler I knew said that postwar Baghdad had become the cheapest place in the world to buy beautiful women. "It's like Czechoslovakia was in '86, '87," said the hustler, whose name was Samir. "That place was full of beautiful girls you could hire for next to nothing."

Over coffee and cigarettes one afternoon, a minor racketeer chatted about business: "Well of course, these are the days where everybody does what they must for the money. A lot of people are, what do you say, like in France, the *putains*? [Expletive] for money! There is a lot of [expletive] for money. Oh my, yes. If a man likes a girl, he will set her up in a little apartment, give her some money, and she will be a *putain*, but in a discreet way. No one will know about it except a few people—and me.

"Of course, there is a lot of stuff going on no one knows about. Everyone is very nervous these days. Especially they are nervous about Uday. He is all over town and when he comes into a place, everybody looks down. Nobody wants him to see them. Because if he sees you and he doesn't like you, he will kill you just like that. He is crazy. When he starts beating someone, he cannot stop with just an arm or a leg. He goes on and on until the person is crippled or dead. And Uday is getting richer and richer all the time. He has two newspapers now, *Babel* and *Rafidain*, and that is a lot of money.

"But getting back to the [expletive] thing. You know, we have in Muslim a concern about a girl if she is not *vierge*. For me that is not a problem, I don't like *vierge* anyway. Too stupid. But many men, if the girl has been [expletive] by some other men before, they will not marry her. In ordinary times, this is not so big a problem, because the young men marry the young girls when they are still *vierge* and everyone is happy. But the wars have killed very many young men who were married. Now their wives are all without husbands, but they are no longer *vierge* anymore. So it is very hard for them to find new husbands. No one wants them because they have been [expletive] by other men. So what can they do? They work in a factory or in a shop, that is not very much money. But if they become a girlfriend to Uday or one of the other big shots, they can get a lot of money, enough in one month to live on for a year. There are a whole lot of apartments not too far from here, in a nice neighborhood near the ministries, that are just for Uday's girls. He keeps a girl in one of the apartments and he [expletive] her for ten days, twenty days, a month. Then he throws her out, but he gives her maybe one-thousand, two-thousand dinars, maybe ten-thousand dinars. And so she is happy enough."

Inflation, plague-like, had swept through Iraq, destroying and transforming. The official rate of exchange for the Iraqi dinar was one dinar for $3 American. The black-market rate, which was the one everyone really used, was more than thirty times that; depending on the day and the dealer, $1 would buy as many as twelve dinars.

Doug Broderick, the field director of the Catholic Relief Services in Baghdad, had made up a chart and hung it on the wall of his office in the Palestine Hotel. The chart showed the increases, in real terms and by percentage, of basic food items since the 1990 invasion of Kuwait: bread up 2,857 percent: infant formula 2,222 percent; flour 4,531 percent; eggs 350 percent.

"What you get with prices like this," Broderick said professorially, "is a Darwinian effect. The rich and the strong survive, the poor and the weak starve. In any society, the very weakest people are the children, so mostly it is children that die. The number of child deaths during the fifteen months of sanctions I would put at between sixty-thousand and one-hundred-thousand. Now, the normal number of deaths would be about thirty-thousand in that time period, based on the normal rate here of thirty-nine deaths per ten-thousand and the births recorded in this time. So, in essence, the infant mortality rate has at least doubled and possibly tripled."

Al Qadissiya General Hospital, a featureless concrete square with 325 adult beds and 130 pediatric beds, serves the 750,000 people who live in the poorest part of Baghdad, Saddam City. The office of the hospital director was down a long, windowless hallway, and everything in the office—the carpet, the furniture, the paint on the walls—was worn and permanently dirty. As if he didn't want to clash with the decor, the hospital director wore old polyester slacks and a laboratory coat that had been stained too many times, so that it was, while more or less white overall, subcutaneously mottled with patches of faded red and brown and gray.

"Really, nowadays, most medicine is not available at all," he said. He was a small, round-shouldered man, and he sat humped over his little glass of steaming tea, as if he were trying to draw strength from its fumes. The lines of his face all drooped exaggeratedly downward, like a hound's. "There are no antibiotics to speak of, no cough syrups, no bronchial dilators, no blood-pressure medicine, no heart medicine, very few anesthetics. Really, it is very difficult for us." He was especially worried about a lack of tubing to deliver intravenous fluids. "We have reached the point now where we are canceling operations because of the lack of intravenous tubing," he said. "And because of this lack too, we are forced to treat all but the most serious cases of malnutrition and diarrhea as outpatient cases."

The director took me for a walk through the wards to see the malnutrition cases. On one bed lay Ala Husein, a girl of 105 days. Her mother sat with her (all the mothers stayed with their children at this hospital, sitting with them all day, sleeping on the floor or in bed with them at night), and she explained the situation. She fed her baby Isomil powdered milk, and since each tin of Isomil lasted three days, she required ten cans a month. Before the economic sanctions imposed by the United Nations, Isomil cost six-hundred fils per can, so that a month's supply cost six-thousand fils, or six dinars. Now, Isomil cost fifteen dinars per can, so that a month's supply cost one-hundred-and-fifty dinars. Her husband's pay was two-hundred dinars per month, and they had six children.

While her mother talked, Ala Husein lay completely still, and a fly crawled on her face. A doctor pulled apart the soft little blankets in which she had been swaddled (tied around her, with a ribbon of cloth, like a papoose) and held up her wasted legs, pinching the flesh. "As you can see," the doctor said, "there is not only no subcutaneous fat left, there is also no muscle left. Look at this chest." He thumped gently on the rib cage sticking out against the skin in sharp relief. "There is nothing left on these bones. What happens in malnutrition, you see, is that the child eats itself. First it eats the fat, then it eats the muscle. When there is nothing left for it to eat, it dies,"

We walked through the crowded wards, stopping at this bed and that, examining this little shriveled-up husk and that little sack of bones and skin. One little boy the doctor unwrapped had feces of an improbably vivid green, the shade of pesto sauce, smeared about his bottom and legs. "They call this 'hunger stool.' Very frequent in these cases. The bowel movement is watery and it is green."

The dying-baby epidemic made Doug Broderick so angry that his face twisted up when he talked about it. "The terrible thing is that Iraq is, technically, overfed," he said. "The food stocks are at 120 percent capacity, 70 percent of which is imported, 30 percent homegrown. But the Government will not distribute the food, or allow anyone else to. They are only giving out 25 to 30 percent of what is necessary for the people to be decently fed. We—Catholic Relief Services—have 1,400 metric tons of food in this country right now, sitting in warehouses, waiting to be distributed. We cannot distribute that food because the Government will not allow us to. They have blocked us from distributing it through the existing network of women's and children's health care centers.

"They could cope with this if they wanted to. But who wants to be seen coping with it? That would be a message they do not want to send. It they sent that message, it would take pressure off of the United Nations to lift the sanctions. The fact is the sanctions make Saddam strong. He can take the time to get rid of his enemies, take care of the Shiites and the Kurds, while his people are busy pointing their fingers at the U.S. and looking for food. Everybody in the country is too preoccupied with food to think about rebellion. The whole nation is dreaming about a nice dinner."

Samir, the Jordanian hustler, was the very picture of his type. He was lean, and fidgety always, even when sitting. He was not handsome—the skin on his face was too large-pored, his mustache was scruffily trimmed, and he had only a middling chin—but he had large brown eyes that shone with an insistent and entirely misleading sincerity, and I thought he was one of those men women wonder afterward how they ended up in bed with. He wore flashy clothes: wool and silk sport coats with overpadded shoulders and pleated pants and Italian loafers. Yet he was unmistakably, irredeemably seedy.

One night he and I sat up late in my room at the Sheraton Ishtar, finishing the last few inches of whisky in a bottle, and he talked of the great days at hand. "I remember what I told my father when I asked him for the money," he said. "Opportunity only knocks once. It is true. This is my one opportunity knocking. After all, how many times in my life are you guys going to sanction this place?"

Samir's father, who owned a car dealership and a soft-drink franchise in Amman, had seen the truth in that, and had bankrolled him, at the end of the war, with $300,000—to run goods from Amman to Baghdad and to sell them for what the market would bear. Business had been good. . . .

"I have made so far $400,000," Samir said. "Whisky, cigarettes, beer, lightbulbs, whatever. But do not sit there and think it has been easy. No, it is a very tricky business. Very tricky indeed. The big problem is that there are too many businessmen here at the same time. Iraqi, Jordanian, Lebanese, Egyptian, Saudi—they have come from all over to be in on the game. And everyone is looking for the same score at the same time. Now, the way you score is to see the need, the shortage, before everyone else does. Let us say you spot a shortage of razor blades. So you drive like hell to Amman and buy up razor blades and bring a truckload down here, and sell them for thirty times what you paid in Amman. Not so damned bad, eh?

"Now, how do you spot the shortage? By going around the city and looking in shops, talking to people, seeing what there is not much of, or what items the prices are going up on. But here is the problem. This city is full of unscrupulous bastards who are hiding all sorts of items in warehouses, to make artificial shortages and drive up the price, and then they bring them out and sell. Maybe they open the warehouse just at the time you bring in your stuff and—bang!—the market is glutted. This happened to me a few times. For instance, about two weeks ago I saw Heineken beer, which is very hard to find. So I go to Amman and bring back three container loads of Heineken. I get here, what do I find? This bastard has socked away two-hundred container loads of Heineken in warehouses and suddenly let them out in the four days I am gone. The shortage is over, the market is glutted, the price is steady again, and I cannot find anyone who wants my beer. So now I have three container loads of beer sitting in a warehouse that I have to pay rent on and I cannot sell and maybe some Government bastards will come steal it in the night.

Even the matter of being paid is a problem. Let us say you conclude a deal for two million Iraqi dinars. Well, you cannot take payment in anything other than twenty-five-dinar and five-dinar notes. Everything else in phony. Once, I was offered payment in American dollars. The best, I thought. I was told they were fresh from the central bank in Kuwait City. Very good. The deal is almost done, I have examined the money; it looks good. I am just counting one last time and I notice—just by the merest chance—one last thing. On every note, all the serial numbers are exactly the same. That is the kind of thing I have to worry about."

"So you make a deal for two million dinars, and let me tell you, two million dinars in twenty-five- and five-dinar notes is a big amount of money. It is paid to you in a rice sack, or a flour sack, and there are many problems with doing business this way. You walk out of a business establishment with a sack on your shoulder, and everyone knows you are carrying a sack of money. Now, a sack of Iraqi dinars is not such a valuable item in Amman or New York. But in Baghdad, where the average person is making a salary of 150 dinars a month, it is a lot of money. So you are a very tempting target. And there is not a goddamn person in this town who does not have a gun. So you can see, it is the kind of thing that is a problem.

"Then, let us assume you get safely to your office. You now have to count the money. You know how long it takes to count two million dinars in twenty-five- and five-diner notes? I have ten employees here in Baghdad who do nothing but count money. They do it all night long, every night, and we still can't keep up.

"But to hell with all that," he concluded, lifting his glass. "By God, I love America, and thank you! By God! Do you know I always said—my whole life—I had one goal, to be a millionaire by the age of forty. And do you know—thank God for America!—if these sanctions last three more months, I will make it."

The woman with the workingman's hands was on her fourth cup of coffee and fourteenth cigarette.

"Sometimes I wonder why I stay. I am rich. I could go. My last letter from my sister in Paris, she said, 'Why do you not come? But I wrote her and said I could not go. I cannot leave my country now. I cannot. I believe that if I stop going on, if I leave my country, my country is defeated.

"Saddam and George Bush, they have together tried to defeat us, each in his own way. George Bush could have sent his army to Baghdad and killed this bastard Saddam, and he did not. We all thought democracy would save us. Now, I do not believe in democracy. I don't believe in anything. Except God. He will save us because there is no way he will allow good people to be destroyed by evil.

"And, of course, Saddam and his criminals, those bastards, are stronger than ever. The only people left in the army are people who are loyal to Saddam. He has given them all new cars and more land and new medals. They know that if anyone else took power, they would disappear from the face of the earth. You must realize this is a class of people who were scum, who came from families that were scum. Their fathers were scum and their father's fathers were scum."

She lit another cigarette, inhaled, grimaced. "It is as if both sides—the Americans and the criminals of Saddam—are using us to work out their experiments. And they are interesting experiments. It is fascinating to see what it takes to bring about the total degradation of a people.

PAUL WILLIAM ROBERTS

Saddam's Inferno

VIRTUALLY EVERYONE in Baghdad has lots of money. And from the moment last fall when I first changed a hundred-dollar bill on the black market, I had a lot of money, too. The Iraqi dinar used to be worth about three U.S. dollars—back when the countries were on speaking terms—but now, officially, there are one-thousand dinars to the dollar. Unofficially, the exchange rate is whatever you want it to be, a factor largely determined by however much you want to carry. At 1,800 dinars to the dollar, I received for my first C-note a Marlboro duty-free bag full of cash in rubber-banded slabs. I felt like a criminal.

PAUL WILLIAM ROBERTS *is a filmmaker, television writer, and author of several books, including an account of his hilariously ironic Baghdad trip,* The Demonic Comedy *(1998), from which this excerpt is taken.*

Then I realized that even

kids selling cigarettes on the street had high rollers' wads stuffed into every pocket. So did the beggars. Wherever I looked there were people carrying shopping bags full of money. In Baghdad, cash registers have to be emptied two or three times an hour. Money is piled on ledges, tossed into old boxes, shunted aside like garbage. People have lost all respect for the stuff. Although a 250-dinar note has recently been introduced, the largest denomination generally available is still the one-hundred, with its picture of Saddam Hussein disguised as a genial, confident banker printed on paper as frail as a dead moth's wings.

The worthlessness of the dinar was why everyone wanted my dollars. Everyone was a money changer. Before long even government officials were offering to change my money at rates ranging from 2,200 to 3,500. This means that the one-hundred-dinar bill is now worth about three cents and the more common twenty-five-dinar is worth . . . nothing. It also means that people are confused, frightened, desperate. Those in the private sector don't know what to charge for anything. Cabdrivers take whatever you give them without even the feeblest attempt to get more. A pack of Marlboros is three-thousand dinars in the morning, then later on the same man in the same place asks for two-thousand. But in the vast public sector, the pullulating Iraqi government bureaucracy where incomes are fixed, the situation is infinitely worse. A good average monthly salary is four-thousand dinars, a sum that now has the same buying power as one dollar, a sum that will get you two packs of Sumer Filters. And in Iraq everyone still smokes: it's not lung cancer that frightens them. Fear rules, assisted by uncertainty. And in between is the parliament of anger.

"My people very angry with you," a cabdriver announced angrily.

"Me?"

"Why you hate Iraqi people? Why your planes bomb our cities?"

I convinced the man that I was Canadian, not American, that my planes hadn't bombed Iraq's cities.

He softened. "Why they make this embargo, hmm? Why they make us suffer?"

The so-called United Nations embargo is much on people's minds, viewed as the prime cause of their current distress: something has to take the blame. But recent history confuses them. There was euphoria during the stomping that was the Gulf War—I was here then too—because everyone felt certain that the slaughter meant the end of Saddam. Iraqis hate Saddam more than we do, and they desperately want to see the end of him. Instead, though, they saw him return in apparent triumph from the war—in Iraq it's called the "Gulf Standoff" (the "Gulf War" was the Iran-Iraq bloodbath)—and witnessed thousands of civilians killed by the 96,000 tons of explosives dropped during the 126,645 allied air sorties or by the 322 Cruise missiles launched at them. Then they found themselves reduced from oil-age affluence to grinding Third World poverty by the U.N.'s trade sanctions. I don't understand this discontinuity, and neither do they.

Baghdad was never an attractive city, but it used to be a great swaggering monument to Iraqi oil wealth and Saddam Hussein's overweening ambition to be the undisputed leader of the Arab world. I once asked him whether he viewed himself as a second Nasser. "No," he replied, in tolerable English. "I am first Saddam." He was right about that. Now Baghdad is as weary as he seems to be—he hasn't given a press conference since 1991—filthy, rundown, squalid. It's been patched up since the allied bombing, but there are more patches than pieces left, and at its best it's about as convincing as Michael Jackson's face.

When the Iraqi Embassy in Ottawa invited me to attend the Seventh International Babylon Festival, I assumed there was a catch. And indeed there was. The day I was due to leave, a fax arrived from Hamed Youssef Hamadi, Baghdad's Minister of Information and Culture, announcing that "a nation-wide referendum for the nomination of President Saddam Hussein for the post of President of Iraq will be held in Iraq on October 15, 1995. . . . The occasion will be both a historic and major event that takes place in Iraq for the first time. . . ." It went on to promise me a glorious month of absolute freedom on the government's tab in "one of Baghdad's luxurious hotels." All I had to do was pay my own way to Amman, Jordan.

If you were invited to Washington but told to fly to Montreal, you'd expect an explanation for the inconvenience, but either General Hamadi assumed that everyone knew you can't fly to Baghdad anymore or he found the task of explaining why the Saddam International Airport hasn't seen much business lately too embarrassing for words. Still, I was convinced that after forty-two hours of continuous travel there would be a lavish welcome in Baghdad. Saddam would do us proud. Pride still means much in the Arab world, and, overlooking the swagger, I also remembered Baghdad as a proud city. Alas, no more. In the words of a Serbian diplomat I met—and he should know—Baghdad is now a "hole of shit."

I was supposed to be staying at the Meridien Hotel, but no one knew where it was, largely because the place was now called the Palestine Hotel. Yet the Palestine had no room for me, indeed had no room for the lobbyful of Mongolians ahead of me. Instead, I was directed to the Sheraton. No one knew where this was either, largely because the place was now called the Ishtar Hotel, although it stood directly opposite the Palestine. The Ishtar had plenty of room, however. In fact, I appeared to be the only guest there. But apart from determined little cockroaches, room was all it had.

Behind the door to 1414 lay a chamber that gave the distinct impression of having been submerged in stagnant water for several months and then kiln-dried. The only functioning light was a terrifying five-foot column containing several fluorescent tubes that sucked what little color was left in the floor, furniture, and walls into a throbbing sheen of raw electricity. Something or someone had been slaughtered at the foot of the bed, judging by a vast magenta stain. A very big cigar had once been allowed to incinerate itself on top of the television, leaving an inch-deep trench in the plastic casing. Above the bath was a jagged hole in the ceiling large enough for a man to climb through. Slabs and shards of plaster still lay in the tub. And deep within a multihued blizzard, believe it or not, Disney's *Aladdin* was actually playing on the only TV channel I could find.

Scheherazade and her Thousand and One Arabian Nights, Sinbad the Sailor, Ali Baba and his Forty Thieves, Aladdin and his lamp—they all called Baghdad home. They all existed only in someone's imagination too. People are hard-pressed to name anyone famously associated with Baghdad who isn't fictional. The once-illustrious Saatchi brothers, Sultans of Slick, the ad-and-marketing wizards who got Britain to vote for Margaret Thatcher and then vote for her again—they were born in Baghdad, which is worth remembering, because no city has a more profound connection with the business of promotion and public relations. The very name "Baghdad" conjures up Essence of Arabia: crowded souks, the robes and turbans, the intrigue, the magic. Yet Baghdad has never really been that romantic place it still occupies in Western popular imagination.

When it wasn't being stomped into rubble by the Turks, Baghdad was being stomped into rubble by the Persians or Mongols. And when this wasn't happening, it was rebuilding itself in preparation for another stomping by Turks or Persians or Mongols. Virtually nothing remains of the city built by Caliph Al-Mansur in the eighth century and glorified by his grandson Al-Rashid, except their names. What little there is that isn't named after Saddam Hussein is named Mansur or Rashid—from cigarettes to hotels and even whole boroughs—because there hasn't been anyone else nonfictional in Baghdad for 1,200 years worth naming anything after. Those caliphs who weren't stomped helplessly into the rubble generally limited their achievements to the fields of body count and heavy demolition. By these standards, Saddam is a conservative, traditional ruler who is still wary of the Turks and Persians but with Americans now filling the threat vacuum left by Mongol decline. And, like his antecedents, he finds Babylon more impressive than Baghdad.

Babylon: where Hammurabi assembled the earliest known legal code; where Nebuchadnezzar held the Israelites in captivity for fifty years; where Belshazzar had his feast and saw the writing on the wall; and where, a millennium and a half after Hammurabi, Alexander the Great died at the age of thirty-three, having conquered the known world and been declared a pharaoh by the priests of Egypt. Here were names and deeds once known by every schoolchild around the globe. Who recalled Al-Mansur? Besides financing a book of fairy tales, what did Haroun Al-Rashid ever do? Saddam has clearly seen the writing on the wall. Hence the Seventh International Babylon Festival.

Nothing remains of Hammurabi's Babylon, however, and not much remains of the city that Nebuchadnezzar rebuilt and made universally famous for its wealth and power and major deity. Unfortunately, quite a lot remains of the city Saddam has been assiduously "reconstructing" for the last fifteen years. The Amphitheater of Alexander the Great, for example, where the Babylon Festival's opening ceremonies and main events were staged, is nowhere near the ruins of Alexander's original building. And the peculiar Bauhaus-Babylonian structure high on a hill beyond the Marduk Temple—beyond the city itself—was Nebuchadnezzar's palace.

"No, no! No photographs of that!" shrieked my official guide.

She had long since convinced me that someone in her position could get into truly dreadful trouble for letting visitors get out of control, so I didn't question her objections and instead photographed the palace when she wasn't looking. The official reason you weren't supposed to photograph it was "because it's forbidden." The unofficial reason was that Nebuchadnezzar's palace was also Saddam Hussein's palace, or one of them: he has scores of others scattered around Greater Baghdad, and a few more still under construction were pointed out to me. Apparently he doesn't like to spend more than two nights under the same roof. Or woman.

Some years earlier I'd met some French architects working on the Babylon reconstruction project who swore on their lives that Saddam roamed around Nebuchadnezzar's palace at night alone, communing with the spirit of the very late monarch, a man in whom he found much to admire—especially the capturing-of-the-Jews bit. If Saddam ever finds Aladdin's lamp the chances are that his first wish will be for a second Babylonian Captivity. The

Babylon Festival's poster had Saddam's profile beside (but on top of) Nebuchadnezzar's profile. Below them both was an announcement, "FROM NEBUCHADNESSAR TO SADDAM HUSSEIN . . . ," which then trailed off into drivel about glorious jihads. Every brick of the new Babylon has stamped upon it "The Babylon of Nebuchadnezzar Rebuilt During the Reign of Saddam Hussein."

Every brick of the old Babylon also had stamped upon it cuneiform information along the lines of "I AM NEBUCHADNEZZAR, KING OF KINGS. LOOK ON MY WORKS YE MIGHTY AND EAT YOUR HEARTS OUT. . . ."

"Look, sir! See?" asked Babylon's own official guide. He'd just levered up one of the stones in Nebuchadnezzar's Processional Path with an improvised crowbar to show me the bird's feet runes of its cuneiform inscription.

I assumed the message pecked into this ancient slab of stone did not say MADE IN IRAQ. Few people can read cuneiform, however, and judging by the translations these few people have made, it is not unjust to suggest that no one can read cuneiform—unless those who wrote cuneiform were semiliterate.

"You like?" the official guide inquired.

I examined the rock more intently, nodding.

"You take it, yes? One dollar Amerkan. Okay?"

I now have eight cubic inches of Nebuchadnezzar's Babylon—a signed first edition—helping to quiet a dreadful, geriatric rattle in my fax machine. For less than a hundred grand I could probably have had Marduk's Temple in my garden.

You have to laugh.

For the first few days I certainly had to laugh. I laughed at the lightbulb shortage; I laughed at the toilet-paper shortage; I laughed at the worthless money; I laughed at a food shortage that had the Ishtar's breakfast chef making three dandruff-thick omelets from one egg, and its lunch and dinner staff chopping a tomato and a green pepper so finely that they provided enough "salad" to cover six plates; and I laughed my way through the acrylic propaganda in the Saddam Art Center. I laughed at the Babylon Festival's opening gala too.

Led by Iraq's token civilian and all-purpose spokesman, Tariq Aziz, twelve Saddam clones, who turned out to be the twelve most senior generals from the Revolutionary Command Council, swept into Alexander the Great's Amphitheater with great pomp and some three hundred heavily armed guards, several of whom stood on-stage the entire evening with their machine guns poised for action. They were all pink and old, these generals, and their old eyes betrayed the toll taken by living with the constant expectation of meeting that bullet or mine or bomb or knife with your name on it. If it seemed somewhat unwise to have 98 percent of Iraq's government sitting in one spot, it seemed still less wise to let off a thousand firecrackers, Roman candles, rockets, and aerial bombs the moment they sat down. Their guest of honor—the leader of Nigeria or some other corrupt cesspit—certainly thought so. He shot three feet into the air, losing his turban in a flurry of robes and arms. I crushed a full pack of cigarettes involuntarily and could feel the fizzing adrenaline frying my follicles an hour later. The generals all laughed, or oscillated their mustaches, pretending they'd been expecting this little faux blitzkrieg to happen. But they clearly had not, and it bothered them. I imagined them suddenly regarding what they'd first viewed as an honor as, in fact, a sign of their eminent expendability in the Leader's eyes.

After all the pomp and gravitas, I would have been surprised not to hear the speech that followed. An exceptionally nasty little general trotted down from his perch and did a creditable impersonation of Adolf Hitler for half an hour, while informing us that the demons in Washington and Israel had better wise up before it was too late. Iraq had, apparently, been patient for the last few years rather than crushed into submission. But Iraq's patience, though formidable, was not limitless. Pretty soon, it seems, Iraq is going to lose its patience and be obliged to stomp both Washington and Israel into rubble. God will lend a hand, though the responsibility for this unpleasant but necessary task mostly rests upon the enormous shoulders of Saddam Hussein himself. And at every mention of the NAME—and there were many such mentions—the crowd spontaneously roared out approval. Or seemed to. In fact, like TV yack shows, there were people planted throughout the amphitheater to incite this spontaneity. I just hope the Pentagon realizes that Iraq is almost out of patience, that we could all wake up any day now to find Saddam informing us that it is finally too late: Iraq has lost its patience and is henceforth and until further notice going to run the planet, as it did long ago, in the beginning, when it was the "Cradle of Civilization" or "Mother of All Chattels," or whatever it was.

After all the pomp, gravitas, and now this crock, I expected we were in for some weighty drama, not a four-hour pantomime that resembled a collaboration between Andrew Lloyd Webber, Beatrix Potter, and the scribes of Melrose Place on a theme of Sex, Brawls, and Ballet in Ancient Babylon.

By the time Young Nebuchadnezzar (who resembled Saddam Hussein about as closely as some makeup genius could possibly manage to make a 120-pound, fine-featured, eighteen-year-old ballet dancer look) had overcome impossible odds and countless burly rivals to wed his queen (a fifty-year-old diva built like the prow of a schooner) I was weeping with laughter. I'd seen Siamese-twin dragons actually catch fire onstage; I'd seen a squadron of three-hundred-pound ballerinas trample a man disguised as a spider to death; I'd seen four men who resembled George Harrison clutch their wigs while performing the cancan through a slaughterhouse of bodies; I'd seen a giant clam devour two girls dressed in aluminum foil; I'd seen an artificial waterfall burst apart and flood the stage while a troupe of giant scorpions performed an ancestor of the square dance; I'd seen the brassiere of a woman with breasts like zeppelins burst apart, taking the top half of her dress with it.

I kept trying to come up with an analogy: on the eve of an election that will grant him a fifth straight term in office and in which he is the only contender, Ronald Reagan invites the entire world to watch a musical version of the American Civil War penned by Dr. Seuss and Hildegard von Bingen, in which the lead role is played by the artist formerly known as Prince, with Elizabeth Taylor as his love interest and the Village People playing the Confederate Army. . . .

The absurdity of it all suddenly illuminated the bottomless gulf between the two countries, however, and it was no longer so funny. Fellini nudged aside Mel Brooks; the clowns laughed while drawing their ice picks. My analogies were not so far-fetched, I realized. Here I was in a country whose leader cheerfully announced the referendum to elect him leader without even a hint of any opposition candidate or alternative. A NO vote presumably meant that you did not want a leader. Yet it was all done with the utmost seriousness, not a shred of irony, not a glimmer of mirth—like watching Monty Python's *Macbeth* and figuring out only halfway through that it was the straight version, that John Cleese as Mac really was out of his tree and that the trees of Birnam Wood really were an army of executioners.

The fear creeps up on you.

I hardly noticed, as I joined five-thousand other people trying to exit Alexander the Great's Amphitheater through one modest door, that a gaggle of Japanese Kabuki dancers were tiptoeing around the stage arranging props. The Japanese were not scheduled to perform that night, I learned later, but they had insisted on performing all the same because they were so appalled by conditions in Baghdad that they'd decided to leave the next morning no matter what—though not with people saying that the Japanese didn't honor their commitments. . . .

I tried to see the funny side of it all on the bus ride back to Baghdad, but I could no longer see what I'd ever found funny about any of it. This was a nightmare from which 20 million people couldn't wake up. The hotel didn't serve atrocious food: it couldn't afford to buy anything better. It hadn't run out of toilet paper either: there was virtually no paper of any sort left in the country. Even the daily propaganda sheet was published only once a week now, if that often. Pharmacies had almost no medicine, and what medicine there was had soared in price beyond the reach of all but the richest. The only people not affected by the embargo were Saddam and his inner circle—the only people it is presumably supposed to affect.

"Then they should just get rid of Saddam," said an editor at one of the world's most prestigious newspapers, when I suggested that an article condemning the U.N. sanctions as inhumane would be appropriate.

He should go over and tell them how to achieve this feat because they'd be eager to learn. I suspected I wasn't hearing measured opinion, though, but unofficial policy. After all, the only way these sanctions can be justified is by firmly believing in the iniquity of the Iraqi people as a whole—and, of course, of Saddam in particular. But it's just another Big Lie. After the laughter came the tears.

They started when I met a woman whom I will call Ala and took her to lunch. She asked me how old I thought she was—small talk, I assumed—and I replied, "Thirty-seven or eight," thinking forty-five or fifty. I was shocked to discover that she was only twenty-six. Then, for the dessert that did not exist in the Ishtar's restaurant, I offered her a chocolate bar. She bit off a tiny piece and promptly began to cry.

"I don't feel right eating it myself," she told me before I'd asked. "Do you mind if I take the rest back for my brothers and sisters?"

Chocolate was not something they'd seen in a long while. They hadn't seen milk in a long while either. That candy bar would cost her over three weeks' wages, I learned. She didn't even think about such "luxuries" anymore. Sugar was another luxury. But the biggest luxury was her job: thirteen people depended on her three-thousand dinars a month. One sister's husband had been killed "in the war" (which one I didn't ask); another sister appeared to be "a single mother"; and besides an unaccounted-for brother all the other siblings were too young to work. Her father had "given up looking for a job." Once he'd owned a construction business and they'd lived in a "nice neighborhood," but now they were down to selling off furniture, and "Father" had seemingly just lost the will to go on.

It was only after half an hour of listening to this tale of woe that it occurred to me I shouldn't be hearing it at all, that it amounted to treason in Saddam's Iraq. I think it occurred to Ala around the same time.

"Please," she said, "this is between us, yes? If they find out, I am finished."

I crossed my heart and swore on my life. But I'd heard nothing yet. In the following days I heard more and more—until I wished there were no more to hear.

The unaccounted-for brother, I eventually discovered, was in prison. He'd originally been charged with what struck me as the noncrime of borrowing money for his business from someone who'd stolen this money. That was how the brother had explained it, I presumed, though he'd probably stolen the money himself. Yet as a defense it was pitiful. Surely he could have come up with something better. It was this very pitifulness, however, that eventually convinced me the story was just as she told it.

Ala had gone to the police station to bail her brother out the day he was arrested. The police chief had a better idea: she would become his third extant wife and her brother would skip out of jail a free man. But Ala was already engaged. When she told her father what had happened, he hit the roof and marched down to the prison to give the police chief a piece of his mind.

"Fine," the chief apparently said. "You'll never see your son again."

A whole catalog of spurious charges was suddenly added to her brother's original sin, and within a week he'd been sentenced to twenty-six years in the Baghdad pen.

Ala didn't need to convince me that prison in Iraq was not quite the same as prison the way we know it. The first time she visited her brother he'd been strung up on a meat hook with his arms tied behind his back for three days.

Hundreds of cigarettes had been stubbed out on his chest and legs. There appeared to be no reason for this punishment besides the fact that it had struck someone as a good idea.

Currently he was sharing a cell designed to hold two people with twenty-three others. The floor was the only toilet facility available; and the only food he got to eat was what his sister and mother brought on the two weekly visits they were allowed. The only possible way out of this hell involved lawyers and money—far more money than anyone could now dream of ever having.

I assumed Ala would soon hit me up for this cash. But she didn't. She also seemed somewhat embarrassed that her brother was in jail, as if it reflected on her. Over the next few days I gradually came to learn that her embarrassment was related to something else altogether.

At eighteen she'd been raped by Lieutenant General Hussein Kamel, Saddam's son-in-law—who'd defected to Jordan a week or so before I arrived. When Ala's fiancé discovered she wasn't a virgin, he broke off the engagement, leaving her that worst of all possible creatures in the Arab world: a woman of questionable reputation, a woman no man worth marrying would ever marry. . . .

It soon became obvious that the "authorities" were not happy that Ala and I were spending so much time together while I was supposed to be attending the "Official Babylon Festival Program." She was worried I might tell someone what she'd told me.

"If you do, I'm finished. You understand?" She drew a forefinger across her throat.

I had been assigned a guide-cum-driver: Faisal.

"Be careful of him," Ala whispered. "He's Mukhabarat."

Secret police, in other words. In a maximum security state like Iraq, there are a good many secret police, backed up by legions of informers, snitches, and those just trying to save their own skin. Even Juvenal's query about who will guard the guardians has been addressed here: one branch of the secret police concerns itself solely with spying on the other branches. Fear is the glue that holds Saddam's labyrinthine state structure together. No one can be sure who the spies are: a father? a husband? a son? your neighbors? And then there are the video cameras in statues, on rooftops or window ledges, watching, always watching. As William Burroughs observed, "A paranoid is a person in possession of all the facts. . . ."

The following day, inadvertently, I did something very foolish. Avoiding Faisal, I took a cab to a bazaar I'd wanted to visit. Paying the driver, I realized I was at the wrong bazaar and walked straight through it to hail a cab at the other end. Failing to find the bazaar with this cab, I noticed the Juma Shaie, a traditional Arab tea shop I'd been to before and liked. So I decided to abandon my search and get out. No sooner had I sat down in the smoky antique cavern and ordered tea than a nervous, scholarly old man in the remains of what was once a good suit asked in French if he could join me.

His name was Wathik, and he'd been educated in

France. He rhapsodized about Paris in the old days for a while, then recounted his life as a teacher in Baghdad. Now he was retired, with a pension of three-hundred dinars a month. I thought I'd misheard—that's about ten cents—but he nodded in anguish, saying that a pack of cigarettes cost him six-hundred dinars. He'd sold all his furniture, sold all his possessions, in fact, and now lived "like an animal." He'd seen me in the tea shop the day before, he claimed, and hoped I might come back.

I asked why, assuming he was about to request a loan.

"You must be my voice," he said, suddenly frightened and desperate.

I offered him my pack of cigarettes and asked how much money he needed. He thanked me profusely, pushing the cigarettes back and taking out a pouch of hand-rolled ones.

"I am used to these," he said. "I don't want to remember what a good cigarette tastes like." He drew closer. "We don't have long. I want nothing for myself, you understand? I want you to tell the world what is going on here. This government is a sham; they are criminals, bank robbers. The highest level of education any of the leaders has is grade four, you know. Now it is like an animal in a cage, this leadership. It is frightened and dangerous. Look around you!" He gestured at the hubbub of backgammon players, tea sippers, and narghile puffers hunched on wooden benches. "They are sheep! Saddam has destroyed the education system; everyone is stupid! And they feed on each other like cannibals! That is what this criminal has done to our land! With his hundreds of palaces and his

Swiss bank accounts. . . . Please!" He grabbed my hand. "You must carry my words around the world."

I told him that no one imagined Iraq was Shangri-la, or that Saddam was the Wise and Bounteous One.

We had to be careful, I was warned: the tea shop owner was a "detective" (I assumed this meant "spy"). And, right on cue, the owner, Muhammad, came over and offered me a tour of his premises, which had been in business since 1941 (and looked it). Muhammad spoke only Arabic, so Wathik trailed along as the proprietor showed me a sulfurous room where the tobacco for narghiles was being prepared in clay cones. It looked like tar and straw.

"It is the worst tobacco," Wathik muttered. "Only sheep smoke it."

When we had dutifully marveled at the wonders of the tea shop and returned to our table alone, Wathik told me that General Hussein Kamel was one of his nephews. I assumed this meant that he had been happy to see Kamel defect to Jordan, but it did not. The whole defection, Wathik assured me, was a plot by Saddam to divide the opposition.

It seemed to be doing just that, since some exiled Iraqis had by now gathered around Kamel as a good figurehead to lead an anti-Saddam coup, while others wanted nothing to do with a man whose past was so questionable and tainted.

"They planned all of this, Kamel and Saddam. It was also a way of hiding some of the billions he has looted from this country. Please! You must be my voice: no one should trust Hussein Kamel."

There was some possibility of truth in Wathik's assertion, because Kamel had formerly had access to Saddam's foreign banking arrangements and had been in charge of the military's nuclear program and had reportedly shifted millions of dollars out of the president's offshore accounts into his own before leaving. He was also married to one of Saddam's daughters, who had accompanied him to Amman.

Listening to this and to more dire indictments of the regime, I became aware of a certain change in the tea shop's atmosphere. The proprietor was on the phone a lot, and a few military types had entered and sat down not far from our table, watching us rather than behaving like customers. It dawned on me that Wathik was the kind of Iraqi whom foreigners are not supposed to meet, that it was a very bad idea to be seen talking with him—bad for both of us.

The old teacher may have been a nervous wreck, but he was not crazy. As fear began to trickle through my veins, I told him he'd better leave.

"I'll finish this tea, then go," he agreed.

Something, however, made me urge him to leave instantly. I felt deeply afraid all of a sudden, and not a minute after he'd gone, Faisal the minder appeared, trying to look casual. He claimed he'd simply been driving by and noticed me inside. I didn't believe a word of it.

Only later did it occur to me that my actions must have seemed suspicious. Changing cabs at the bazaar would have had the appearance of trying to lose anyone following—which I now presume they were—and encountering

Wathik the moment I entered the tea house must have seemed like a prearranged meeting.

My hotel room had been searched, too. I'd expected this from the start and thus employed all the usual tricks for seeing if someone has rifled your belongings. No one had until that night, though. From then on there were two mustachioed men standing in the corridor whenever I left the room. It completely unsettled me, so I decided to spend the next few days attending only official events and, rather than avoiding Faisal, making a point of inviting him everywhere I went.

It's hard to convey this level of fear, this species of mass nightmare. The country's facade had been stripped away, and I could now see the Iraq that Ala and Wathik described everywhere I looked. It was utterly sinister—and just as difficult to leave as it was to enter. Telephoning within Baghdad was hard enough; getting an overseas line was all but impossible. No one knew where I was, specifically, and the British Embassy in Amman had warned me not to enter Iraq in the first place.

"We can't help you there," a consul had stated bluntly. "If you're in trouble, the Russian Embassy is your best bet: they're looking after our business in Baghdad now."

Not very reassuring. At the time I didn't take him seriously, though; now I did.

When Faisal offered to drive me back to Amman for much less than anyone else was charging, I had images of lying squashed and bloody on the highway, an official government telegram dispatched to my home: There has been an unfortunate accident. . . .

I attended all the Babylon Festival events from then on, watching Jordanian sword dancers, Russian Cossacks, Armenian jugglers, Mongolian singers—the whole circus, the lot. And I never even smirked, let alone laughed. There's nothing funny about Iraq. Nothing.

I never thought I'd come to see Jordan as a little paradise, but when my passport was finally handed back by an Iraqi official and I was waved on, out of Saddam's grim republic and into another Hussein's bright desert kingdom, I felt like an exiled soul finally forgiven and summoned back to Life and Light.

It is hard to think of those who still wait so patiently for this privilege, harder still to watch as our governments make their hell still more hellish. In mid-January, I received a letter from Ala. It was unsigned and there was no return address. She left spaces for the English words she did not know. "Pleese," she wrote, "I knowing not where to turn and now have no job. It is very bad now . . . can you help us, Mister Paul. . . . "

RAYMOND BONNER

Always Remember

THERE ARE FOUR million Kurds in Iraq. They make up a quarter of the population, and they live primarily in Dohuk, Irbil, and Sulaimaniya provinces. The region is bordered on the north by Turkey, where the Kurdish population is ten million; on the west by Syria, where there are a million Kurds; and on the east by Iran, where there are five million Kurds. The Iraqi Kurds and the nation's ruling Baath Party have been engaged in almost nonstop warfare—an ethnic war, in essence—since the Baathists consolidated their power, in 1968. The Baathists espouse Pan-Arabism and insist that Iraq must be an Arab state. The Kurds are not Arabs. They have a distinct

RAYMOND BONNER *has been a foreign correspondent for the* New York Times *and* The New Yorker *magazine (from which this 1992 piece was excerpted). He has covered hundreds of stories from Latin America and the Middle East.*

language, culture, and history, and have consistently sought more cultural and political autonomy than the Arab rulers in Baghdad have been willing to grant.

Traditionally, the Kurds, most of whom are Muslims, gave their loyalty not to any nation but to family, clan, and tribe; and it was not until the First World War that Kurdish nationalism emerged as a significant factor in international politics. President Woodrow Wilson declared in the Fourteen Points—his outline of the world order that he envisioned after the war—that the ethnic minorities living in territory previously under Turkish control, which included nearly all of present-day Iraqi Kurdistan, should be assured of "an absolutely unmolested opportunity of autonomous development." For a brief period, it seemed that this part of Wilson's idealistic program might become a reality. In 1920, the Treaty of Sèvres, which dealt with the breakup of the Ottoman Empire, provided that if a majority of the Kurds in what had been southeastern Turkey wanted independence it was to be theirs; the treaty also said that if they did establish an independent state then Kurds in a part of the Ottoman Empire known as Mosul Vilayet would be free to join it. (Mosul Vilayet, a province the size of Portugal, is today Iraqi Kurdistan.)

But the Kurds never got an opportunity to establish their independent state. In 1923, nationalist forces led by Kernal Atatürk came to power in Turkey and declared that they would not recognize the Treaty of Sèvres or any other agreement entered into by the Ottoman leaders. The Treaty of Sèvres was superseded by the Treaty of

Lausanne, which was signed by the Turkish and the Allied governments in 1924. It made no mention of the Kurds. About a million and a half Kurds found themselves inside Turkey, and half a million more in Mosul Vilayet. Then, in 1925, the League of Nations ceded Mosul Vilayet to Iraq, which had come into being when Britain and France carved up the Middle East after the war. During the twenties and thirties, rebellions arose throughout Kurdistan, but they were quelled. The only time the Kurds have ever had their own state was just after the end of the Second World War, when those in the Mahabad region of Iran established the Mahabad Republic. It survived only eleven months before the Iranians crushed it.

In Iraq, Kurdish nationalism did not emerge as a potent political movement until the overthrow of the monarchy, in 1958. The new rulers legalized the Kurdish Democratic Party, or K.D.P., and the Kurds took advantage of the political freedom to begin demanding some degree of autonomy. But the government adopted a republican constitution that more or less guaranteed conflict between the Arabs and the Kurds: although one provision recognized the rights of the Kurds, another declared that Iraq was an Arab state. In 1961, war erupted between the Kurds and Baghdad.

Throughout the 1960s Iraq was torn by coups and countercoups, and various factions, hoping to gain power or to hold on to it, sought the support of the Kurds. In 1970, Saddam Hussein, who was the strongman in Iraq's Baathist government but was not yet president, agreed to meet the demands of the Kurdish leaders, in order to placate at least one potential enemy. "When he is weak, he gives away everything in order to survive," says Latif Rashid, who has been a Kurdish political leader since the seventies. "When he is strong, he takes everything."

Among other things, the 1970 agreement provided that Kurdish would be the language of instruction in schools, along with Arabic; that government officials in the Kurdish region would have to speak Kurdish; and that Kurds would be brought into the central government at senior levels. In principle, the agreement gave the Kurds more autonomy than any other Iraqi government had ever granted them, but it was never put into effect. Saddam "had no intention of carrying out either the letter or the spirit of the agreement," according to John Bulloch and Harvey Morris, British journalists who wrote *No Friends but the Mountains*, a 1992 book about the Kurds. "Instead he was intent on consolidating Baath Party power and needed a temporary halt to the destructive war in the north. . . ."

In early April of 1987, in what was probably the first major deployment of chemical weapons by the Iraqi government against its own people, the Iraqi Air Force dropped chemical weapons on several Kurdish villages in Irbil province. (The notorious chemical bombing of Halabja, in Sulaimaniya province, which left at least four thousand Kurds dead and brought Iraq's use of chemical weapons to the attention of the world, occurred the following year.) Among the villages that were targets of the April

1987, attack was Shekh Wassan, fifty miles northeast of the city of Irbil, which is the capital of Iraqi Kurdistan.

"It was a quarter of an hour before dark," Abdullah Kadir Asad, a resident of Shekh Wassan, told me in June. "I saw a dozen planes. They bombed the first time there, behind the village." He pointed toward some high ridges. "And then they dropped them in the village. We saw people vomit, and they felt blinded; their faces were dark, and their skin had blisters."

At least fifty people were killed by the gas, most of them women and children, And more than four hundred were injured. "Nobody knew what it was, because it was the first time with chemical weapons, and we did not think the government would use chemical weapons against us," I was told by Nadir Sadiq, a villager whose mother, father, and wife had died from the poison.

Abas Ali Mahmoud, who is now twenty, was away from his village when the attack came, and he rushed home to check on his parents. While he was searching for them, he heard a woman crying for help. Inside a stone house, he found the woman, her daughter, and her father and mother, all of them blinded. He led them down a valley to a paved road four miles away. "When I got to the main road, helicopters came, and I told these blind people to run, but they couldn't," he recalled. The helicopters began shooting at them. The older man and woman died instantly; one of the younger woman's hands was severed by bullets, and she died later. The child was eventually found and taken to safety by other villagers. Mahmoud did ultimately find his own mother, but his father had disappeared. All that Mahmoud knows about what became of his father is that he was taken to Irbil.

The morning after the chemical attack, people from nearby villages came to Shekh Wassan and helped the injured down the valley to the village of Sorochawa. Among them was Ali Aziz, aged thirteen, whose grandmother had been killed in the attack. "When the bomb landed here, I became blind," he told me. "I couldn't see anything. My skin was hurting me—I felt as if it had been removed from the rest of my body." He pulled up his shirt to reveal a large light-colored blotch on his stomach. "Still now I am sick. I cannot breathe well. And I cannot walk as usual. My stomach and all my body pains me." At Sorochawa, soldiers gathered the injured and took them first to the town of Ranya and then to Irbil. "They told us they were taking us to a hospital." Instead, they were taken to the headquarters of Amn, Saddam's internal-security department—a large compound in the center of Irbil—and put in its jail. There the villagers were told that if anyone asked who had dropped the chemical bombs they should say that it was the Iranians. Aziz recalled, "One day, a security man came to the hall and shouted, 'Who attacked you with chemical weapons?' No one answered, because we were too afraid. He said, 'You have to say that Iran did it.'"

The prisoners were given no medical care and very little food—rice and soup once a day. Many people were so sick from the gas that they couldn't eat even that, Aziz said.

The people of Shekh Wassan have compiled a list of the villagers who died, either directly from the chemical bombs or later in the Irbil jail. There are more than a hundred names on it—infants, teenagers, men and women in their sixties and seventies.

One day not long after the people from Shekh Wassan were taken to the jail in Irbil, security officials chased everyone away from a cemetery a few miles south of the city, near an asphalt factory. Then a large government truck arrived. It contained the bodies of twenty-six Shekh Wassan villagers, the driver told Bakir Asad Omar, the cemetery guard. The bodies were tossed into a pit that had already been dug by a bulldozer. The villagers do not know where most of their other relatives and neighbors are buried.

Between seven hundred and eight hundred nameless victims of the security forces and the military were buried in the Irbil cemetery in 1987 and 1988, Omar said as we walked among the weeds and thistles. "Shaqlawa," he said, pointing to a row of mounds, each marked by a piece of concrete; next to them were regular graves, with tombstones. Shaqlawa is a summer resort in the mountains, between Irbil and Shekh Wassan. The Shaqlawa victims were brought in a large military truck one morning in February of 1987, Omar said. There were twenty-two of them, all men, in their teens and twenties. They had been blindfolded and their hands had been tied behind their backs.

Omar pointed to another area and said that ten bodies were buried there and then to an area where forty-two bodies were buried. He does not know how any of these people died. He said that when there were a large number of bodies they had arrived in military trucks, but when there were only two or three they arrived in ambulances. Whenever someone died in the custody of Amn, which often meant that he had been tortured, the morgue at one of the hospitals in Irbil was asked to issue a death certificate so that Amn could show it to relatives who might inquire. On one occasion, the Irbil office of Amn sent a hospital a letter asking for death certificates for seventy-seven "criminals," whose names it listed. One hospital worker entered in a secret ledger the names and ages of the victims whose bodies Amn sent with requests for death certificates. On November 14, 1987, fourteen bodies were brought to the morgue; on April 12, 1989, sixty-four arrived. More than three hundred people are on the hospital worker's list. The overwhelming majority of those listed are males between the ages of seventeen and thirty-five. No one believes that the list is anywhere near a complete accounting.

As documents such as these indicate, the operations against the Kurds were not those of a state run amok but those of a state operating with extreme efficiency according to rules that it had established. The government itself kept meticulous records. When, for example, a man named Bakhtiar Qoron wrote to the Sulaimaniya government to inquire about the fate of his father, Qoron Ahmad, and his mother, Naima Abdulrahman, a file was opened and given a number—24900. The file contains a letter from an "interrogating officer." He wrote that Ahmad and Abdulrahman were the parents of the "criminal Hushyar Qoron Ahmad, a member of Iran's agents, who was apprehended together with eight other agents after they conducted sabotage activities and assassinations. . . . They were all turned over to the Revolutionary Court, in Case Number 47/1987,' and were hanged "at 7 P.M. on 12 July 1987."

The interrogating officer added that Qoron Ahmad and Naima Abdulrahman were "liquidated on 19 May 1987," and that the regional security office "was informed by our letter [marked] Secret and Personal . . . 17980 dated 25 May 1987." This liquidation, the interrogating officer notes, was carried out "in compliance with the order from the Struggling Comrade Ali Hassan al-Majid," which had been sent "by the letter Number 106309' dated 1 May 1987 marked Secret and To Be Opened Personally regarding the liquidation of first degree relatives of criminals." ("First-degree relatives" means parents, siblings and children.)

On another occasion, a woman named Bakizah Omar Said inquired of the General Security Directorate in Baghdad about one of her relatives, Barham Omar Said Muhammad. Baghdad sent a cable to the Sulaimaniya Security Directorate asking for information. In reply, the Sulaimaniya director of security said that Barham Omar Said Muhammad was an Iranian agent who had participated, along with four other "criminals," in the assassination of a member of the Baath Party. The Sulaimaniya officer explained that the Secretariat for the Northern Planning Bureau had by letter No. 6806, dated December 12,

1987, decided that it was "appropriate to cut off the heads of family members of three of the criminals, including the family of the criminal Barham Omar Said Muhammad." As for Barham Omar Said Muhammad and the other "criminals," the Sulaimaniya security officer advised Baghdad, "At 1:15 P.M. on 24 October 1987, the aforementioned criminal and his fellow criminals were executed by a firing squad." The execution had been supervised by several public and Baath Party officials, he noted, and was "broadcast in our governate."

Executions were indeed videotaped and broadcast to the public. One broadcast shows three young men, blindfolded and gagged with black cloth, tied to eucalyptus trees. They are then executed. A man in uniform goes to the three victims' bodies, which are bullet-riddled and slumped over, and delivers a final shot. Off camera, people who have been brought to witness the execution applaud.

On August 20, 1988, a cease fire in the Iran-Iraq War went into effect, and Saddam immediately began moving troops to the western part of Kurdistan. Within a week, thirty-eight infantry brigades, two armored brigades, thirty artillery detachments, and at least one chemical-weapons battalion were engaged in concentrated attacks on villages in Dohuk. The offensive there was part of what Saddam called Operation End of Anfal—the final phase of his Operation Anfal.

Operation End of Anfal began with chemical bombardments. "On August 25, 1988, in the early morning, we saw about eight planes moving around," a farmer named Hamed Hassan Saleh told me in June as we walked through the Dohuk village of Birjinni. "One of them bombed here on this side." He pointed to the western edge of the village. "The bomb looked like a watermelon coming from the end of the fighter plane. We saw the smoke. It rose about sixty meters. It was white smoke. It smelled like apples." Birjinni sits between two ridges. On the west side of the village are three shallow craters, thirty yards apart. Each crater is about eight feet in diameter, and in each is a canister about two feet in diameter and three feet long. The canisters are twisted and rusted and have no visible markings. On the slope of the ridge just to the north are three other craters, containing the remains of other canisters. Altogether, twelve canisters are believed to have landed in and around the village; it has since been determined that the principal chemical that the Iraqis used against the Kurds on August 25 was mustard gas mixed with nerve gas. The Iraqi military dropped gas on more than fifty villages on that and following days.

When the lethal fumes drifted across Birjinni, women and children started crying and screaming, and everyone ran toward the nearby springs and streams, having been told by the *peshmerga* that in the event of a chemical attack they should wet pieces of cloth and cover their noses and mouths. Hamed Saleh, himself a *peshmerga*, grabbed his wife and their five-year-old daughter and nine-year-old son, and they ran to the east side of the ridge, away from the smoke. When the attack started, his son Dejwar was at the house of Hamed's father, a few hundred yards below Hamed's house; Hamed's mother and his ten-year-old sister were also there. In the ensuing panic, the family got separated. Hamed Saleh recalls, "I cried with all my might, 'Where are you, my father? Where are you, my mother?' My mother cried, 'We are here!'" His eyes were stinging from the chemicals and he felt weak, but he managed to reach his mother and sister; they were near a stream and had covered their faces with wet cloths. They couldn't see, and his mother's tongue was swollen. "I threw my sister in this stream," he told me. He kept searching for his father and Dejwar, and soon found them under a big oak tree three hundred yards below their house. Their faces were blue. His father had not covered his face or the boy's. "He was too old, he didn't understand," Hamed Saleh says. He himself was so weak from the effects of the gas that he wasn't able to move his father, and other villagers helped him carry the old man and Dejwar to a spring. "When we reached it, they were without life," he said.

In the valley below Birjinni lies a small village called Koreme. This village was not hit by chemical bombs, but the people could see what was happening in the mountains above them, and they began to flee through the mountains to Turkey—through the same passes and along the same roads that vast numbers of Kurds would take in March of 1991, when the Kurds once again rose up against Saddam. Thousands made it to Turkey in 1988, but not all did. Soldiers had sealed off the road and the main passes.

"We saw soldiers everywhere," Abdulkarim Naif Hassan, a farmer from Koreme, told me. He and many of his neighbors headed back to Koreme, but it was now occupied by army soldiers and by *jash,* as Kurds who joined Saddam's preliminary units were called. (The name means "little donkey" in Kurdish.) Hassan went on, "When we got close, the *jash* called to us, 'Come back! We are Kurds, like you, and there is an amnesty for you.' We went to them. We were happy. They gave us water and cigarettes."

Between three hundred and four hundred of the villagers surrendered. From this group the soldiers singled out thirty-three men. Villagers recalling the incident four years later were not sure if all thirty-three had had weapons, but most of them probably did have rifles of some kind. One of the Iraqi officers, a lieutenant, got on the radio and called a command post at Mengish, a small town two miles west of Koreme. The lieutenant reported capturing thirty-three men who had tried to escape to Turkey. Hassan recalled that the lieutenant asked, "What should we do with them?" Then the soldiers marched the thirty-three over a small rise. The soldiers had told the men's parents, wives, and children, who remained behind, not to worry—they were just going to ask the men some questions, and the men would later join them in Mengish.

On the other side of the rise, the soldiers ordered the prisoners to form a line, starting at an almond tree and extending down a slope toward a stream. "Now I realized that they had brought us here to execute us," Hassan said. He was eighteen years old at the time and had been a *pesh-*

merga for two years. "They ordered us to squat down and to get close to one another." The grass was tall, up to the men's knees. Seventeen or eighteen soldiers stood about fifteen feet away," on slightly higher ground. The lieutenant gave the order to fire.

When Hassan heard the order, he threw himself forward, onto the ground. One bullet grazed his jacket at the shoulder, another his baggy pants at the hip. No bullet touched his flesh. After the soldiers emptied their magazines, an officer gave one of them orders to go down the line of men and shoot each with "the blessed bullet." Hassan was under several bodies, and the final executioner missed him. "It was a miracle," my interpreter commented as he listened to Hassan's story. Hassan and three others who survived the firing squad hid in the valley for ten days. Then they surrendered to the *jash* in another village, and eventually they were sent to an internment camp. While they were there, Hassan married, and his wife gave birth to a son; he named him Najbeer, which means, my interpreter said, "always remember."

The men, women and children, who surrendered in Koreme were taken to a military fort in Dohuk, a city of three hundred thousand that is the provincial capital. The fort is about two hundred and fifty yards long and a hundred yards wide; it has thick walls thirty-feet high; the windows are small and barred. At each corner is a turret, with observation slits for sentries. The Kurds call this structure and other like it castles.

At Dohuk, the refugees were given only one piece of

bread a day and water from a military tank truck that was brought into the courtyard; the water was hot. The men were tortured. "I was beaten until I was unconscious." Hassan Merza Osman, who was fifty years old at the time, told me in Koreme. "I can show you the signs of the beatings." He raised his shirt to reveal long scars on his back. The soldiers also put lighted matches to his beard, he said. "We all saw it," a young woman near him said.

They were sitting in the grass on a warm summer day this past June, on the edge of the mass grave where the soldiers had buried the young men of Koreme after executing them in 1988. The bodies in the grave were being exhumed by an international team of forensic anthropologists, and relatives and friends who had come back to the village waited pensively. Osman's wife, Fahima, a black-and-white-checked scarf wrapping her narrow face, yanked up grass with her right hand, gathered it in her left hand, then threw it aside. Only a foot or so beneath the grass were the remains of two of their sons, Salam and Saleh. Salam was twenty when he died, the father of a one-year-old son and a three-month-old daughter. Saleh was sixteen; his wife was pregnant. When the digging was finished for the day, a teen-age girl named Khayira sat alone in the alpine meadow, the long grass scattered with scarlet poppies, yellow dandelions, and tiny white wildflowers. Khayira's father was buried in the grave. So were two of her brothers, one of whom was thirteen years old when he was shot. After a while, her aunt, Najma, came and sat next to Khayira; strands of gray hair among the black showed at the edges of her white lace scarf. A dozen or so children gathered; a small girl had a garland of delicate white flowers in her hair. "All we have is God," Najima said softly to her niece. "May God show mercy." They wept, quietly. The earth contained the body of one of Najima's brothers, fifty-three years old at the time of his execution. It also held the bodies of two of her sons; they were fourteen and sixteen.

Back in 1988, after a couple of weeks at the Dohuk fort, Najima and Khayira, Fahima and Osman, and the other Koreme villagers who had survived the bombings and beatings and executions were loaded into vehicles and driven a hundred miles southeast, to a place called Beharke.

"Every day, there were a hundred and thirty, a hundred and forty, a hundred and fifty vehicles," a man named Najat Muhammad, who was living nearby at the time, told me. These were military and civilian trucks of all sizes, commandeered from all over Iraq. The torrent of trucks jammed with people lasted twelve days—and then "nothing more," Muhammad said.

Beharke is on a plain twenty miles west of Irbil. There were no houses, no tents, no water there when the Kurds arrived. They had no food, and the government gave them nothing. When the people of Irbil, a city of more than five hundred thousand, heard about the newcomers' circumstances, they mobilized a relief effort. The better-off went through their closets and kitchens and gave away what they didn't need. A hotel owner donated a large sum of money. Collection centers were set up. Car caravans stretched for miles all day long from Irbil to Beharke. They brought kerosene, lamps, clothes, medicine, beds, pillows, towels, oil, sugar, tea, flour, and water. The people of Irbil got the donations to the internees by bribing the soldiers.

"If the people from Irbil had not bought us food, we would have all died," Hassan Merza Osman recalled. Many of those taken to Beharke think that that was what the government wanted. "The soldiers told us, 'We're not bringing you here to survive, but only to die,'" another Koreme villager said. As it was, hundreds died, or maybe thousands; no one knows for sure. "Every day, people were dying—four, ten, fifteen—continually," another man from Koreme told me. "We dug the graves and buried them."

On a knoll just to the west of Beharke is a cemetery on the site of a former village called Jeznikan, which was levelled by the Iraqis during the 1980s. Forty or fifty of the graves are marked by stone slabs bearing the name of the deceased. Rocks are scattered about the rest of the knoll, and from a distance it looked to me like a field that had not been cleared for cultivation. Up close, however, I saw that the rocks were in fact simple grave markers. As I walked among the graves, my interpreter commented, "Most of them are children. . . ."

The most fundamental issue for the international community is the Kurds' relationship to Iraq. If Kurdistan is to remain an autonomous region, how much autonomy will it have? Or are the Kurds to became a federated state within

Iraq, which would give them still more control over their lives? And the ultimate question is whether they will break away altogether and become an independent nation. It is hard to imagine a people with a greater right to nation-state status than the Kurds. In a 1912 paper for the Council on Foreign Relations the historian and papyrologist William Westermann wrote, "The Kurds can present a better claim to 'race purity' [ethnic unity] and continuity of cultural pattern and for a longer period than any people which now inhabits Europe." Kurds trace their roots back four thousand years, and Kurdistan encompasses an area larger than Italy. An independent Kurdistan would also be economically viable. . . .

Most Kurds are baffled by United States policy. They understand that Turkey is allied with the West, but they don't understand why that alliance is so important that the suppression of Iraqi Kurds should be allowed to continue. They understand that sanctions are needed against Saddam, but they don't understand why the Kurds should suffer because of them. Over and over, I was asked how it was possible that the United States went to war for Kuwait, which isn't a democracy, but is willing to do so little for Kurdistan, which is struggling to become one. And the Kurds find it difficult to understand why the United States is opposed to independence for the Kurds when so many other ethnic nationalities are gaining their freedom.

"Here we are at the end of the century, and we are facing a world community that says, 'Don't talk about a separate state. Don't disturb the boundary with Iraq," Fouad Baban, a doctor who was one of the founders in 1991 of the Kurdistan Human Rights Organization, said. In negotiations during the past year between the Kurds and Baghdad, the Iraqi government has said that it will give the Kurds essentially the same autonomy that the government offered in the seventies. "The majority of the people won't accept that," Dr. Baban told me. "The final solution, the democratic solution, is independence." Three other doctors and a lawyer, all members of the Human Rights Organization, were sitting next to him. We were having dinner in the garden behind the Salam Hotel in downtown Sulaimaniya, and they all agreed with what he said.

I asked them what would happen if Saddam were to be deposed and Iraq were to become a democracy. Would the Kurds then be satisfied with something less than independence? This hypothetical question assumes a lot—not only that Saddam would be ousted, which is possible, but also that Iraq itself would become a democracy, which it has never been, and that a new Arab government in Baghdad would treat the Kurds as equals. Nevertheless, it is a proposition that one hears frequently from Western policymakers.

"If Saddam is out of power, then a federation as two equal republics—this might be a reasonable solution," Dr. Baban said.

I posed the question about democracy and limited independence repeatedly when I was in Kurdistan, and the answers I received can be summed up like this: Yes, if Iraq were to become a democracy Kurdistan would be willing to accept a federated status. But then the person answering would add "for now" or "for the time being."

The international community might not have to face a demand for Kurdish independence immediately, and maybe not for ten years, or even for another generation. But, unless one refuses to recognize the dramatic world events of the past two years—in the former Soviet Union, in Yugoslav—one must realize that eventually the Kurds will demand their independence, and will quite likely take up arms to get it, if that is the only way. But the makers of foreign policy are rarely farsighted, and politicians don't think past the next election. Washington, therefore, is not, at the moment, entertaining the notion of an independent Kurdistan. Instead, it tells the Kurds to negotiate with Baghdad.

TONY HORWITZ

In the Land Without Weather

ON A MIDSUMMER'S night in Baghdad, soon after an Iraqi triumph in its eight-year war with Iran, Muhammad Abid stood outside his restaurant by the Tigris River, poking a net at the last fish circling in a tiled tub of water.

"Tonight Iraq celebrates victory and eats a very great deal," he said. But in the morning, maybe we find that peace is like this fish, a slippery thing that swims round and round and sneaks away."

TONY HORWITZ *is a Pulitzer Prize-winning journalist and staff writer for* The New Yorker. *He is the best-selling author of books including* Blue Latitudes *and 1991's* Baghdad Without a Map, *from which this excerpt is taken.*

Snaring the river fish, Muhammad flopped it onto the sidewalk to see if it was of suitable size for my dinner. Then he picked up a rusted monkey wrench.

"We must never forget," he

said, raising the tool in the air, "that Iraq has enemies everywhere."

"Persians." Thuuunk.

"Syrians." Thwaaap.

"Zionists." Thluuub.

He gutted the bludgeoned fish with a few deft strokes and propped it over a wooden fire. "No one," he said, wiping blood on his apron, "makes love to Iraq."

No one loves to visit Iraq either—certainly not three times in one summer, as I did in 1988. Baghdad was for me the most depressing of Middle East cities, though it had once seemed the most romantic. The name conjured images of a fantasy Arabia, a land of harems and slave dens, of Sinbad the Sailor and Ali Babi. It was the sort of place I imagined traveling to aboard a magic carpet.

The actual journey resembled walking through the gate of a maximum-security prison. Iraq Air officials in Cairo told me to report four hours preflight for security, and I needed every minute. Guards frisked passengers from toe to turban while X-raying their bags to the point of radioactivity. Then the soldiers lined us up on the burning tarmac to identify our luggage while they shook us down yet again before we boarded the aircraft.

Every personal effect was regarded as a potential weapon. One passenger had a small bottle of cologne, and the guard uncorked the perfume and passed it beneath the man's nose, presumably to see if it was chloroform or some other substance that could be used to disable the crew.

The guard asked for my camera, aimed it at me and clicked, checking, I guess, for a gun inside the lens. Then he plucked the penny-sized battery from the camera's light meter and pocketed it; the Duracell could somehow be used to detonate bombs.

"You are lucky," said the Egyptian in line behind me. "Last time I flew, you could not carry on anything, not a book, not a pen, not even a diaper for the baby. It was a very boring ride."

At the airport in Baghdad it was my typewriter that aroused suspicion. Iraq requires the licensing of typewriters so security forces can take an imprint of the keys to trace antigovernment literature. Behind the customs desk rose a ziggurat of other forbidden imports: videotapes, audio cassettes, binoculars—any instrument for gathering or disseminating information. Even foreign blood evoked xenophobia. The first sign welcoming travelers at immigration stated that anyone who failed to report for an AIDS test would be imprisoned. There was a certain irony to the sign, as few Westerners visited the country. Iraq didn't issue tourist visas. Never had.

The second sign—and the third and the fourth and the fifth—showed the jowly, mustachioed face of the Iraqi president, Saddam Hussein. Big brother was watching from portraits on every wall surrounding the baggage claim. He was watching from a leviathan billboard outside the airport—Saddam International Airport. He was even watching from the dial of the wristwatch worn by an official sent to the airport, to watch me as well. "Saddam is like Superman," the official said, showing how the watch hands ticked across the leader's cheeks and brow.

The man pointed me to the back of a government sedan. As soon as I climbed in, windows eased up, locks clicked shut. We nosed onto a four-lane highway toward the city, past a huge sports stadium, past huge modern mosques, past huge billboards of Saddam, illuminated in the night.

My escort worked for the Information Ministry, which, by definition, made him a poor source of information.

"Is this near the presidential palace?" I asked as we passed a heavily guarded compound.

"Not far," he said.

"And where is the Foreign Ministry?"

"Also nearby."

Searching for neutral topics, I commented on the weather. Yes, he said, it is very hot. How hot he could not say. The weather in Baghdad was classified information, "for security."

We pulled up on the street in front of the hotel. Concrete pylons blocked the driveway. Pylons blocked the entrance to every hotel and government building we'd passed: security against car bombers. As the locks clicked up, I asked my escort if I needed to check in at the ministry the following day.

"It has been arranged," he said.

In the hotel room, Big Brother gazed out from the television screen as a chorus of voices sang in the background:

"We will challenge them if they cross the border, oh Saddam.
The victory is for you, oh Saddam.
With our blood and with our soul
We sacrifice ourselves for you, oh Saddam."

In Iraq, paranoia comes with the territory. The arid Mesopotamian plain has been overrun repeatedly by foreign armies: Greeks, Assyrians, Persians, Mongols, Turks, and now Persians again. It was this last incursion that I'd come to report on. Or rather, it was the war's recent turn in Iraq's favor that had prompted Baghdad to grant my months-old request for a visa.

Iraq never acknowledged that the war had ever tilted the other way, though it had for five or so years. The morning's *Baghdad Observer*, a slim and Orwellian paper, devoted the upper half of its front page to a picture of the president, as it did every day, apropos of nothing. Alongside the picture, War Communiqué No. 3221 announced that Iraqi troops had "liberated 13 strategic mountain peaks at the northern sector" and inflicted "thousands of enemy casualties." The enemy's original taking of the now-liberated peaks had never been reported. In eight years of war, no Iraqi defeats and no Iraqi casualties were ever reported.

At the Ministry of Information, Mr. Mahn, director of protocol for the foreign press, sat behind his desk with a red flyswatter in one hand and my requested "program" in the other. The fat, flyswatting official reminded me at first of Sydney Greenstreet in the movie *Casablanca*. Except that Mr. Mahn looked even more like Saddam. It was an unspoken rule that officials not only draped their walls with Saddam portraits and wore a Saddam watch, but also mimicked the president's squarish haircut and think, well-manicured mustache. Unfortunately for Mr. Mahn, Saddam had recently decided to lose weight, and officials across Baghdad were now on what was known as the "Saddam diet." Officials' target weights were published, and those who failed to lose the proper weight lost their jobs instead. By my third visit to Iraq, Mr. Mahn had shed fifty pounds.

I'd been warned of the difficulty of seeing Iraqi officials and had listed every person I could think of on my program, beginning with Saddam Hussein. Mr. Mahn took out a red pen and crossed out the president's name. "His Excellency, of course, is too busy to see you," he said. Saddam's face was everywhere, but the man himself was elusive; he'd held one press conference for the Western press in ten years.

"This is no," Mr. Mahn said, crossing out the next official I'd requested.

"This is also no." He continued down the list, alternating strokes of the red pen with slaps of the red flyswatter.

"This is no." Thwap.

"Never mind.

"No.

"Still no." Thwap.

"Never mind."

After five minutes, Mr. Mahn had squashed a dozen bugs and reduced my epic-length list to three or four requests. One of them was to "see current fighting on the southern battlefront."

"This maybe you can see," Mr. Mahn said. "On video." He stuffed the list into his breast pocket. "Now you can go back to the hotel and wait. We will see what we can do with your program."

Wandering back to the hotel, shielding my eyes against the blinding sun, I seemed to be touring a city-wide portrait gallery devoted to a single subject. The traditional Islamic ban on representation of the human form had been overcome in Baghdad, in a very big way. Saddam's face perched on the dashboards of taxis, on the walls of every shop and every office, on clock faces, on ashtrays, on calendars, on billboards at every major intersection—often four pictures to an intersection. Some of the portraits covered entire building fronts. And to ensure that your eye didn't ignore the pictures from sheer repetition, Saddam appeared in innumerable guises; in military fatigues festooned with medals, in Bedouin garb atop a charging steed, in pilgrim's robes praying at Mecca, in a double-breasted suit and aviator sunglasses, looking cool and sophisticated. The idea seemed to be that Saddam was all things to all people: omniscient, all-powerful, and inevitable. Like God.

"There are thirty-two million Iraqis," went a popular Western joke in Baghdad. "Sixteen million people and sixteen million pictures of Saddam."

Iraqis didn't tell that particular joke. Article 225 of Iraq's penal code stated rather baldly that anyone who criticized the president, his party or the government, "for the purpose of raising public opinion against authority," would be put to death.

Technically, Iraqis required government permission to chat with foreigners. Those who did so regularly were likely to be questioned by the regime's five security forces, which spied not only on the people but on each other. The first man I approached on the street, to ask the time, held up his arm as if warding off demons and scurried away. More often, pedestrians or shopkeepers responded to my approaches by stating politely that their English, or my Arabic, was not so good.

"People just don't talk to you much, particularly about politics," complained a United Nations worker named Thomas Kamps, who had worked in Iraq for three years. "They know that's the fast lane to the electrodes and the dungeon."

Expatriates in Baghdad made a grim hobby of collecting police-state horror stories. One diplomat's wife had spent much of her two years in Baghdad pushing infants in strollers. She said not a single Iraqi had stopped on the street to smile at her babies or utter so much as a "koochie-koochie-koo." 'They're scared even to be seen talking to infants," she said.

A Turkish diplomat attended the unveiling of a new wing at the arts center—Saddam Arts center. Each time the opening speaker mentioned the president's name there was a twenty-second pause for the audience to applaud. "The speaker mentioned Saddam a lot, and his speech ended up taking an hour and forty-five minutes," he said, yawning in his office the following day.

A Japanese diplomat lost his way one night in the neighborhood of the massive presidential palace. Soldiers opened fire on his car, as they did at any vehicle motoring slowly by, or making a suspicious U-turn in the vicinity of Saddam's residence. "The policy is 'Shoot first and don't ask questions later,'" explained the diplomat, who escaped unharmed. He said two Westerners had been killed at the same spot several years before.

There were genies inside every telephone and telex. A United Nations worker from Ethiopia told of phoning a colleague in New York and switching, midsentence, from English to his native Amharic. A voice quickly cut in, instructing him to "please continue in a language we can understand."

The state forbade direct calls overseas and limited operator-assisted calls to three minutes. Western publications were often seized at the airport, as were short-wave radios. Censorship of the domestic media was total. And ordinary Iraqis were barred from traveling abroad, even to Mecca. Baghdad was airtight, hermetically sealed against the outside world.

At a stall in the city's cramped bazaar, under cover of commerce, I struck up a conversation with a youth named Tariq, who sold Smurf T-shirts and Adidas sweatsuits. "Born in the USA" blared from a nearby boom box, drowning out the tap and clink from the centuries-old copper market, where men crafted giant urns, plates, ashtrays, and wall hangings with Saddam's face adorning the center.

"I not understand you Americans," Tariq said genially. "You make good clothes and music. You have California girls. But you start this war on us to help Israel. Why you do this?"

I tried to explain that most Westerners believed Iraq had started the war. Tariq looked at me blankly. Big Brother was watching from life-sized photos on two of the stall's three walls.

Tariq's neighbor, who owned the boom box, wandered over and began jabbing his finger at me. "He says you can have your Bruce music, you can have it all back," Tariq translated. "Now that we win the war, we not need to beg America for anything anymore."

Back at the hotel, I tried to telex New York, to give an editor a contact number. The telex machine was mysteriously broken. Three hours later, I returned to find other telexes sent, but not mine, "Machine still broken," the operator said. When I complained, a French manager appeared and took me into a back office. The telex operators, he said apologetically, all worked for security and were under strict orders to vet journalists' telexes with the Ministry of Information. It was the weekend and no censors were available.

I used the hotel's Xerox machine. The staff made copies of my copies, "for security." Hotel staff watched me carefully each time I went in and out. I tried to call New York. There were no open lines. In three visits to Iraq, there was never an open line. Apart from the stilted reports of the *Baghdad Observer*—faint crackles of the BBC World Service—I received no news at all of the outside world.

This isolation unsettled me much more than the distance I'd felt in a country such as Yemen, cut off from the world by a Third World phone system and by the genuine remoteness of the place. Here there were touch-tone phones, five-star hotels, and bland modern buildings of steel and glass. But I might as well have been on Pluto. America could vanish in a mushroom cloud and I'd still be sitting there watching Saddam on television as a chorus sang, "The people love you, oh Saddam, and you love the people."

Not all people loved Saddam, of course, and I eventually located a few Iraqis brave enough to speak out. An office worker whom I will call Saleh chatted politely over tea until his colleagues filed out for lunch. Then he turned up a radio and leaned across his desk, speaking in an almost inaudible whisper.

"My phone is tapped, this office is bugged, and for all I know my grandmother is wired for sound," he said. "But sometimes a man must speak his mind. Saddam Hussein, he is the worst dictator ever in the history of man."

Saleh said this with the grim but giddy urgency of a parachutist leaping from an airplane. I could be shot," he added, smiling wanly "for what I've just told you."

Saleh's job required him to write reports, and he'd applied several times for an Arabic typewriter. Each request had been denied, so he'd reapplied for a machine with English characters. He'd been waiting a year. "What am I going to do with an English typewriter?" he wondered, laughing. "Incite tourists to riot?"

Like most Iraqis, he'd stopped seeing anyone but his family and closest friends. "Who else can I trust? Can I even trust them?" And he limited himself to small acts of defiance that would have seemed petty in any other setting. While the walls of most Iraqi homes and offices dripped pictures of Saddam, Saleh displayed nothing more than a calendar adorned with the president's face. But he kept a carpet decorated with Saddam rolled up in the front closet of his home, just in case. "If there is a knock in the night, I can roll it out before answering the door," he said. "A man must be brave, but he must not be reckless.

A few days after my arrival, I was dozing through the afternoon heat when the phone rang. It was Mr. Mahn at the Information Ministry. "We have called this and this and that," be said wearily, adding that item number sixteen on my program had been arranged: an interview with his superior, the Minister of Information and Culture. I had listed the minister as an expendable, to pad out the program, but I could hardly afford to turn him down.

As the first point of contact for the foreign press, Information Ministry officials are often slick, Western-educated bureaucrats, adept at chatting amiably with journalists and offering innocuous statements on almost any topic. They are the governmental equivalent of corporate flacks.

But in Iraq, public relations wasn't very well developed. Arriving on the top floor of the Information Ministry, I wondered for a moment if I'd been sent to the wrong department. The elevator door swished open and I found myself staring down the barrel of a submachine gun. The guard holding it studied me carefully, then led me along a carpeted corridor to an enormous sitting room with a suitably enormous portrait of Saddam. The guard gestured toward a pair of couches, then, when I sat down, he said that I'd taken the minister's seat. It was indistinguishable from the other couch, except that its back was flush with the wall, providing a clear view of the corridor and elevator door.

Another man appeared, clad much like the guard in olive-drab fatigues with a pistol strapped to his waist. He had the stiff bearing and watchful gaze of a secret service agent. He was the Honorable Minister of Information and Culture, Latif Jasim.

Jasim spoke no English, nor did he go in for the usual Arab pleasantries. He also didn't reveal much about himself. Curious about his qualifications as the highest cultural officer in the land, I asked Jasim about his career before Saddam and the Baathist party seized power in 1968.

"I was a party member," he said.

"At university?" I asked.

"Not necessarily."

We moved on to matters of state, and his answers seemed crafted from the pages of the *Baghdad Observer*.

On Iraqi support for the Palestinians: "Israel is an alien body in this region. Science is advancing all the time, and Israel should expect that one day rocks will turn into other things."

On the law decreeing death for those who insulted the president: "We are not in the United States. Your head of state changes every four years. Here we cannot accept a leader being insulted."

On the ubiquitous portraits of Saddam: "The president has nothing to do whatsoever with the portraits. It is a natural and spontaneous thing from the people."

The interview lasted half an hour, during which Jasim managed not even the hint of a smile. He was the antithesis of slick, the last person most Arab governments would wheel out to present a warm and unthreatening image to the Western press.

As the man with the submachine gun saw me to the elevator, I wondered why Jasim took such precautions; after all, there were armed guards downstairs, and concrete pylons blocking the driveway. As usual, the only explanation I received was from a diplomat.

"It's always best to have your own private bodyguard," he said. Iraqi leaders don't have a history of dying peacefully in bed."

The history of modern Iraq reads like *Macbeth,* only bloodier. Since 1920, there have been twenty-three coups, not counting the scores of attempted revolts, such as the one Saddam joined in 1959. Then aged twenty-two, he stood on a sweet corner and emptied his pistol at the car of a military strongman, Abd al-Karim Qasim, who had himself seized power only a year before in a bloody coup that killed Iraq's royal family. Qasim, who was wounded later boasted that he had survived twenty-nine attempts on his life. His luck ran out a short time later and he was executed following a coup that briefly brought Saddam's Baathist allies to power.

Sixteen years, two coups, and many purges later, Saddam muscled his way into the presidency. He celebrated the event by sentencing twenty-two of his closest conspirators to death on trumped-up charges of treason. Saddam served as a trigger man on the firing squad. Ever since, Amnesty International's annual reports on Iraq have read like transcripts from the Spanish Inquisition: prisoners fed slow-acting poison, children tortured into ratting on their parents, teenagers returned dead to their families with fingernails extracted and eyes gouged out. Top generals keep going down in mysterious helicopter crashes, and Saddam has even liquidated members of his own family. The Minister of Information could hardly be blamed for watching his back.

Between interviews, I wandered the streets of Baghdad, which for lack of a better word could be called "sightseeing." It wasn't easy to play tourist in Iraq. There was, first of all, the matter of maps. There weren't any, and hadn't been since early in the war. Like the weather report, maps were banned because they could aid the Iranians in aiming their missiles at the Iraqi capital. Maps could also, of course, aid dissidents in plotting assassinations or coups.

Broad areas of the city were sealed off, including the presidential palace, which flanked a long stretch of the wide and muddy Tigris. You could catch a glimpse of the complex from the eighteenth-floor bar of the Sheraton, but you couldn't photograph it: "For Security Reasons," a sign announced, "It Is Forbidden to Take Photos in This Area." It was also forbidden to photograph animals, which might make the country seem backward. Even photographing Baghdad's premier tourist attraction, a striking memorial to the war dead, could be hazardous. One Japanese visitor had attempted it at night and alarmed the guards with the flash on his camera. They responded with a burst of machine-gun tire, missing the Japanese man but riddling his car with bullet holes.

I went, without camera, to see the war memorial, which is shaped like a huge broken egg and called the Monument of Saddam's Qadissiyah Martyrs. The name says something about the Iraqi mind-set—and about the long memories fueling conflict across the Middle East. Qadissiyah was the seventh-century battle at which Muhammad's general, Khalid ibn Walid—nicknamed "Sword of Islam"—drove the elephant-riding Persians out of Mesopotamia. Saddam's constant invocation of Qadissiyah was a way of reminding Iraqis that their war with Iran was the culmination of a millennial battle against Persian aggressors Like Muhammad's horsemen, they too would ultimately triumph.

On the Iranian side, Khomeini cast the conflict more explicitly in religious terms. He named the repeated Iranian offensives after the Iraqi city of Kerbala, and spoke constantly of liberating both it and the neighboring city of Najaf. Iranians revere the two cities as the burial sites of seventh-century "martyrs"—Ali, Hassan, and Hussein—whose deaths sparked the great schism in Islam between Sunni and Shiite. By invoking Kerbala, Khomeini was reminding Iranians that their cause was no less than a crusade against infidels.

The two leaders had one message in common: both advertised the conflict as a holy war, so those killed in battle were *shaheed*—martyrs—and entitled to a free pass to paradise. After eight years of war, Khomeini had reached Kerbala V, Saddam was busily erecting new monuments to Qadissi martyrs, and a million men had gone off to heaven, leaving the two leaders no closer to victory.

Beneath Baghdad's war memorial was a museum to Saddam's life, including a family tree tracing his ancestry to Muhammad, his birth certificate, and his fifth-grade report card (he scored an eighty-nine in history, his best subject). Not featured, though perhaps more revealing of his childhood milieu, is a pamphlet authored by his foster father, Khairalla Tulfah, titled: "Three Whom God Should Not Have Created: Persians, Jews and Flies." However, there was a photograph of the car Saddam filled with bullets while trying to kill Abd al-Karim Qasim in 1959. Saddam was wounded in the attack and reputedly dug the bullet from his own leg while escaping to Syria. A statue downtown marks the site where the shooting took place. Iraq was the first country I had ever visited that enshrined an assassination attempt as the most glorious event in the nation's history.

The rest of the capital seemed rather drab. As far back

as the twelfth century, an Arab traveler lamented of Baghdad: "There is no beauty in her that arrests the eye, or summons the busy passerby to forget his business and gaze." The flat, sunbaked plain surrounding the city offered little to build with, except mud. Invaders had periodically leveled most of the great buildings that did once exist. And Iraq's vast oil wealth had finished the job, with swaths of the old city ripped down to make space for towering hotels and housing blocks.

To his credit, Saddam also spent much of Iraq's wealth on improving the lives of ordinary people. The onetime Ottoman backwater was now among the more prosperous countries in Arabia, with villages electrified and schools and hospitals dotting the countryside. This modernization, though, was hard to see firsthand. Traveling outside Baghdad required official permission and an official escort. Two escorts, actually. Ministry of Information officials weren't permitted to travel alone with foreigners, as there would be no one to listen in on the conversation.

This arrangement seemed rather cumbersome, so I opted instead for a day trip I could take on my own, to Babylon. The ancient city lies sixty miles south of Baghdad along a dull road bordered by date palms, mud-brick villages, and fifty-foot-high placards of Saddam. Just outside Babylon, I came upon the biggest portrait I'd yet seen. It showed the president receiving inscribed tablets from a skirted Babylonian king, beneath the words "From Nebuchadnezzar to Saddam Hussein."

Most of what was once Babylon has been pilfered by

archaeologists or carted away to provide bricks for nearby towns. The Iraqis have rebuilt the ruins into a kind of fairy-tale castle with gaudy, blue-painted walls simulating the original glazed brick of the Ishtar Gate. A museum inside records some of Nebuchadnezzar's haughty words: "Let everything my hand has made be immortalized for eternity." Not to be outdone, his modern-day heir has inserted several bricks in the rebuilt Babylon, inscribed with the information that they were laid "in the era of the leader Saddam Hussein."

On the day I visited, in mid-June, the temperature was about 110 degrees. There were no other tourists, only a handful of Bedouin hustlers lurking in slivers of shade cast by free-standing pillars. One of them grasped my sleeve and unfolded his fist to reveal a tiny cuneiform tablet and a statuette of a Babylonian king.

"Very ancient," he said. And very cheap, at only ten dollars.

Another man offered to guide me to the Tower of Babel, a short drive away. His car looked as though it had recently been unearthed in the excavations. We stalled beside a mound of dirt, about like your average landfill. "This is Babel Tower," he said, adding in a hushed voice, "You need something old? You need a King Hammurabi?"

Depressed, and depleted by the heat, I drove back to Baghdad through the onetime Fertile Crescent, between the Tigris and Euphrates, as a voice on the radio wailed:

"You are the perfume of Iraq, oh Saddam,

The water of the two rivers, oh Saddam.
The sword and the shield, oh Saddam."

That night I went to visit Muhammad the fishmonger at his restaurant by the Tigris. He was dubbing and gutting fish while the radio reported another advance by Iraqi troops. The war was fast approaching its end, with the borders back to where they had been when Saddam first invaded Iran in 1980.

"Our enemies should not forget," Muhammad said, in a husky imitation of Rambo, appearing that week in Iraqi cinemas, "how we kicked Khomeini's butt."

The restaurant was empty except for four men riveted to a small television set, watching Iraq play soccer in the Arab Cup finals against Syria. Damascus had supported Iran throughout the eight-year Gulf War, exacerbating a long-standing feud between Saddam and the Syrian dictator, Hafez al-Assad. Their murderous rivalry was now being played out on the soccer field.

"This game is almost as important as beating the Persians," Muhammad said.

At halftime, with the scored tied at zero, Muhammad suggested we slip across the street for a beer. Though straitlaced in most respects, Iraq is remarkably unbuttoned when it comes to drink and entertainment. Muhammad's restaurant sat beside Abu Nawas Street, a neon-lit stretch of clubs and bars named for a medieval Arab poet who is famed for his erotic verse.

At one time, hundreds of Filipina and Thai "bargirls" plied their trade on Abu Nawas Street, but Iraqi women, some of them war widows, had recently inherited the trade. "The local talent," Muhammad warned, "is not so good."

We entered the first club just as two doormen carried out a white-robed Kuwaiti, feet first, smelling of whiskey and perfume. The Kuwaitis, barred from drinking at home, were among Abu Nawas Street's best customers and were renowned for being cheap drunks.

Inside, the scene was reminiscent of the New Arizona in Cairo, with men huddled around whiskey bottles as three musicians played an atonal tune on tambourine, drum, and violin. Muhammad picked out a rear booth upholstered with fake red velvet and cigarette ash. It was so dark that I couldn't see Muhammad's face. We were barely seated before a woman squeezed in beside me, whispering in my ear, "Pretty boy want to fickey fickey? Madame good, very good."

Muhammad leaned across the pitch-black booth and lit a match an inch from the woman's nose, revealing a haggard, heavily madeup face and the shoulders of a longshoreman. "By Allah!" he cried, shooing her away.

Muhammad had chosen the dark to attract the bargirls, who collected fifty dollars for a beer and a brief cuddle. As a Westerner, I served as bait. No sooner had the first woman deported than another muscled in, clutching me in a playful hammerlock.

Muhammad lit a second match. "Good grief!" he groaned. "What species is this?"

He yelled at the bartender to bring him "good girls, not so ugly," and the procession continued, though the quality remained the same. In half an hour, Muhammad had exhausted his matches and the supply of women in the bar. A dancer in a sequin dress took the stage and began a vague sort of gyration that was billed as "Oriental dance."

After five minutes of dancing, the woman began singing, and the acoustics were so bad that I couldn't catch a word.

"What's she singing?" I asked Muhammad.

He shrugged. "'We love you, Saddam,' something like this." He scanned the bar for partners. The woman began dancing again, and perfumed, drunk Kuwaitis stood up to shake with her. One tumbled into a giggling heap and had to be carried off the stage by his friends.

Muhammad sank deeper into the gloom. "I not have girlfriend in three years," he moaned. "Who knows. Maybe when the war ends these Iraqi women get married and the Filipinas come back." Draining his beer, he suggested we move on to a club called the Ali Baba.

As we stepped outside, the Arabian night exploded with machine-gun fire. Bright-red tracers streaked across the Tigris from antiaircraft guns positioned on the opposite bank. All Baghdad was celebrating. A guard by the door gave us the news. Iraq had outdueled Syria in overtime, two to one.

Muhammad smiled. "Iraq," he said, "has kicked another butt."

ANDREW AND PATRICK COCKBURN

Saddam at the Abyss

FIFTY MILES FROM the capital, returning Iraqi soldiers could already see the black cloud over the blazing al-Dohra oil refinery on the edge of Baghdad. It was early March 1991, and these exhausted men were the remnants of the huge army sent to occupy Kuwait after its conquest by Saddam Hussein the previous year. Now, routed by the United States and its allies, they were in the last stages of a three-hundred-mile flight from the battlefields. They were crowded into taxis, trucks, battered buses—anything on wheels. One group clung desperately to a car transporter.

ANDREW COCKBURN *is the author of several books on defense and international affairs and has written about the Middle East for* The New Yorker. PATRICK COCKBURN *has been a senior Middle East correspondent for the* Financial Times *and the* London Independent. *This excerpt is from their 1999 book* Out of the Ashes.

Soon they were inside the city, only to find it utterly changed. Just six weeks before, the low-lying Iraqi capital on the banks of the Tigris had been a rich modern city, built with the billions of dollars flowing from the third-largest oil reserves in the world. Expressways and overpasses sped traffic past gleaming modern hotels, government buildings, and communications centers. Lavishly equipped hospitals gave the citizens medical care as good as could be found in Europe or the United States. Even the poor were used to eating chicken once a day. Then, beginning at 3:00 A.M. on January 17, precisely targeted bombs and missiles had thrust Baghdad and its 3.5 million inhabitants abruptly back into the Third World.

There was no power because all the power stations had been knocked out in the first days of bombing. The people of the city huddled in darkness. The stench of decaying meat hung over the more prosperous districts as steaks in carefully stocked freezers slowly rotted. In the hospitals, doctors trained in the finest medical schools in Europe operated by flashlight.

Like any advanced society, Iraq had been totally dependent on electricity. Water came from the wide Tigris River that flows through the city, pumped and purified by what had been one of the most modern and efficient systems in the world. Now a jury-rigged system brought a muddy brown liquid spluttering out of the taps for just one hour a day. Oil billions had given the city an up-to-date sewage system, but the pumps at the treatment plants had been silent since the power generators had been hit, and every day 15 million gallons of untreated sewage poured into the Tigris.

Few cars moved along the streets and tree-lined avenues because the gas stations had long since exhausted their supplies and al-Dohra, along with all other Iraqi refineries, had been smashed in the bombing. In the sparse traffic, black smoke poured from the exhausts of some vehicles, a symptom of watered-down gas available on the black market at a hundred times the prewar price.

Familiar landmarks lay in ruins, like the handsome Jumhuriya Bridge across the Tigris in the city center, now trisected by allied bombs. Surviving bridges had old sacking draped over the sides and little saplings tied to the railings, a vain effort to deceive the computers and laser-targeting systems of the enemy weapons. Symbols of authority, like the Ministry of Justice, at first glance seemingly untouched, were empty shells, their insides gutted by high explosives. The phones had stopped working when two laser-guided bombs had hit the communications center across from the Mansour Melia Hotel and melted the satellite dishes on the roof, isolating Iraqis from the outside world and each other.

The air was full of smoke from the burning refinery and from piles of tires set alight during the war to confuse allied warplanes. The restaurants on Sadoun Street were shuttered and empty, replaced by curbside cooking fires fueled by branches torn from trees by the bombs. Over everything there hung the yellow haze of a winter fog.

Somewhere beneath the gloom was the man who had caused the disaster, President Saddam Hussein, his thoughts and actions, even his whereabouts in those dramatic days, a mystery to his people and to the outside world.

Physically, he had changed since the war had begun. In the months of crisis between his invasion of Kuwait on August 2, 1990, and the start of the United States—led counterattack in January 1991, the Iraqi leader had played to a global audience. Sleek in the beautiful silk suits created by his Armenian tailor, Saddam had sat in his palaces declaiming to visiting statesmen and journalists on the justice of that invasion, defying the international coalition that was building up its forces to oust him.

Now the president of Iraq moved about his capital like a man on the run. Like the rest of the high command, he had been careful to stay out of the underground command bunkers built for the war against the Iranians in the 1980s. He had known that the Americans would carefully target these places and that their bombs could—and did—penetrate the thickest concrete. The bombing had stopped, but still he was sleeping in a different house every few nights, staying mainly in the middle-class al-Tafiya district of the city, quiet because many of its inhabitants had fled Baghdad.

Once upon a time, Saddam had sought to confuse potential assassins about his movements by deploying whole fleets of identical Mercedes, choosing the convoy he would use only at the last minute and dispatching the others in different directions as a distraction. These days Saddam drove only in cheap, inconspicuous cars, accompanied by a single bodyguard—a colonel who himself wore no insignia of rank. The few trusted aides and intimates he visited saw a shrunken figure. He had lost as much as forty pounds in the first mouth of the war. Now the olive-green uniform of his ruling Baath Party hung ever more loosely on him. "I don't know what God will bring tomorrow," he remarked despairingly to one of his intelligence chiefs.

Officially, his government was in denial, issuing statements that the defeat of his army in Kuwait had been a historic victory, that the occupation of that little oil-rich kingdom had been justified, even hinting that Iraq would try again. The few remaining foreign journalists camped on the lower floors of the al-Rashid Hotel (the elevators had long since stopped running) found Ministry of Information censors still routinely changing the phrase "defeat of the Iraqi army in the south" to read "the fate of the Iraqi army in the south" even as Iraqi generals were meekly accepting conditions laid down by the victorious allies.

To the few trusted aides permitted in his presence, the dictator exhibited a greater sense of reality. One of these was a stocky forty-four-year-old general, the chief of military intelligence, Wafiq al-Samarrai, who, like many other ranking servants of the regime, sported a mustache trimmed in the style of his leader. He had made his reputation during the bitter eight-year war with Iran. Saddam valued his professional judgment and had been visiting his emergency headquarters almost every day since the Americans had started bombing Baghdad. (Anticipating that it would be a target, al-Samarrai evacuated his prewar command post days before it was duly crushed by bombs.)

On the day after the allied armies began to sweep, almost unopposed, through Kuwait, Saddam made a rare though roundabout confession of error. "In two hundred years," he remarked to al-Samarrai, "nobody will realize that this was a wrong estimate about what would happen."

"This" had been Saddam Hussein's great gamble in August 1990, that he could surprise the world by seizing the little oil emirate of Kuwait on his southern border and get away with it. The gamble had failed, just as his bet a decade earlier that he could invade his neighbor Iran, then in postrevolutionary chaos, had landed him in a bloody eight-year stalemate. The war against Ayatollah Khomeini had at least ultimately garnered him a partial victory, a de facto alliance with the United States, and the strongest military forces in the Persian Gulf. But the Iran-Iraq war had also cost the lives of hundreds of thousands of Iraqis and, more important for Saddam, had saddled him with $80 billion in debts. Kuwait had been a wager that he could refill his coffers and secure a whip hand over the world's most important oil-producing region, but he had not expected the consequences of losing to be so terrible.

The invasion of Kuwait had been his idea alone. At first it seemed a brilliant success. Saddam's elite divisions had overrun the country in hours, sending the Kuwaiti royal family fleeing over their southern border into Saudi Arabia. The United States and the rest of the world had been caught entirely off guard. As his Republican Guards had massed on the Kuwaiti border at the end of July 1990, the consensus of opinion among those watching his moves had been that he would at worst merely seize part of the northern Kuwaiti oil field and possibly two disputed offshore islands. Later, Deputy Prime Minister Tariq Aziz told an interviewer that this limited invasion had indeed been the original plan. At the last minute, Saddam eschewed this cautious approach and went all the way.

Saddam has often been prone to sudden, unpredictable gambits. At a high-level meeting in September 1979, soon after he seized total power in Iraq, he even delivered a brief homily on the utility of such tactics as a political principle. "What is polities?" the recently installed president asked rhetorically in his slightly shrill voice. "Politics is when you say you are going to do one thing while intending to do another. Then you do neither what you said or what you intended." That way, he suggested, no one could predict what you were going to do.

Along with this taste for sudden rolls of the dice, there was a strong element of fatalism in the Iraqi leader. He once told King Hussein of Jordan that ever since his narrow escape after trying and failing to assassinate Iraqi president Abd al-Karim Qassim in 1959, he had felt that every extra day of life was a gift from God. "I consider myself to have died then," he declared. He acknowledged only one greater power. On a visit to Kuwait after his conquest, he talked to thirty of his senior commanders. A tape of the meeting, later smuggled out of Iraq by a dissident, records him describing the invasion as part of his messianic mission. "This decision to invade Kuwait we received almost ready-made from God," he says. "Our role is simply to carry it out." The audience response was limited to shouts of "God is great."

If Deputy Prime Minister Tariq Aziz, Saddam's perennial voice to the outside world, is to be believed, he did at least try to point out to the leader what the consequences of the invasion might be. In late March 1991, Aziz met with an old friend, the Jordanian politician Zeid Rifai, for the first time since the invasion of Kuwait. "What did you people think you were doing?" asked Rifai. "Didn't you realize what would happen if you seized Kuwait?"

"The leadership made some mistakes," mumbled a slightly crestfallen Aziz, a dangerous enough admission to anyone but an old friend. They both knew who "the leadership" was.

"Well, why didn't you try and talk him out of it?"

"I did," Aziz explained. Just before the Iraqi army crossed the border, Saddam had finally revealed the full dimensions of the plan to members of his cabinet, who were unaware that the limited incursion originally planned had been drastically enlarged. Aziz chose an indirect way to point out to the boss that this could be a perilous undertaking. "I said, 'The Americans may come to Saudi Arabia and counterattack. Why don't we go all the way and take Saudi Arabia too?" In suggesting an even bigger gamble, he hoped that his master might reflect on the hazards of the invasion plan. But Saddam took it straight, gently chiding Aziz for his impetuosity.

"In that circle, the safest course is always to be 10 percent more hawkish than the chief," says one veteran Russian diplomat long stationed in Baghdad. "You stay out of trouble that way"

There was no one left to stand up to Saddam. In 1986, when Iraq was on the verge of defeat in its war with Iran, the professional army generals had secured some leeway in directing military operations. As soon as they had finally won a narrow victory with the active help of the U.S. Navy in the Persian Gulf, Saddam got rid of them. Some were executed, others retired. Defense Minister Adrian Khairallah Tulfah, Saddam's first cousin but widely liked and respected in the army, died in 1989 in a helicopter crash during a sandstorm. It is a measure of the violence of Iraqi politics that everybody in Baghdad assumed that Saddam had arranged for the helicopter to be sabotaged, though the storm was violent enough to blow the roof off the headquarters of military intelligence. Queried by a foreign interviewer about his purges of the military during the Iran-Iraq war, Saddam was less than reassuring: "Only two divisional commanders and the head of a mechanized unit have been executed. That's quite normal in war."

Once installed in Kuwait, Saddam utterly failed to appreciate the game he had started, and continued to overplay his hand. At the end of August, he met Yasir Arafat, the Palestinian leader, and Abu Iyad, Arafat's chief lieutenant, who were in Baghdad in a vain attempt to mediate. "If I make a peace proposal," Saddam told the Palestinians, "then I'm the one who will have to make concessions. If the others propose one, then I can obtain concessions."

But President George Bush, steadily building up military strength in Saudi Arabia, had less and less reason to compromise. Saddam wholly underestimated the strength of the coalition that was about to attack him. Just before the war, be appealed to Arab and Muslim solidarity by, among other measures, redesigning the Iraqi flag to include the Islamic rallying cry "Allah Akbar"—"God is great." Iraq did enjoy popular sympathy in the Arab world, but no powerful friends. Saddam had invaded Kuwait at the very moment that the Soviet Union, Iraq's old ally, had gone into terminal decline. He had failed to understand the military superiority of the American-led alliance, entertaining the fantasy that if there was fighting, his troops could withstand bombing from the air and could inflict heavy casualties on any allied ground assault. In the secret meeting with his commanders in Kuwait before the war, he told them that during allied air raids they should "stay motionless underground just a little time. If you do this, their [bombing] will be in vain. . . . On the ground the battle will be another story"

The truth seems to have dawned on Saddam that war was inevitable only after a fruitless meeting between Tariq Aziz and Secretary of State James Baker five days before the war. Even then, little was done to prepare ordinary Iraqis for war. When allied planes approached Baghdad at 2:58 on the morning of January 17, their pilots were astonished to discover that there was no blackout and that the Iraqi capital was "lit up like Las Vegas." Government ministries were floodlit.

Some of the population still trusted their leader to

avoid war. Trainers at the racetrack in Mansour, a fashionable district full of foreign embassies in the center of Baghdad, were still walking racehorses on the afternoon before the first bomb attacks. No one had any delusions as to what war would mean if it did come. Despite Saddam's bombast about "the mother of all battles," the feeling in the streets was resigned, with few expectations other than the inevitability of defeat. Pro-government rallies in Baghdad just before the war started consisting entirely of schoolchildren assembled by officials of the ruling Baath Party. The largest public meeting in the city in the days before the bombing turned out to be a gathering of pigeon-racing enthusiasts. Nor were the Iraqis ill-informed about the approaching war. There was little on Iraqi radio or television, but people spent hours listening to foreign radio stations in Arabic, switching from the BBC to Monte Carlo to Voice of America. "Our main hobby is listening to the radio," one Iraqi told us at the time. In the days before the bombing, as many as 1 million out of 3.5 million people in Baghdad left the city. They feared that if Iraq fired a Scud with a chemical or biological warhead at Tel Aviv, Israel would respond with a nuclear strike.

At the start of the bombing, an old man drinking tea in a dilapidated café near Nasr Square explained what he thought, using a double-edged story. He repeated the old Koranic tale of how once "the Abyssinians brought elephants to conquer Mecca. At first the Bedouin warriors were dismayed by the strange beast, but God sent birds to Mecca who dropped stones on the elephants and killed them." Saddam himself had recently told the same story, adding that he had only just learned the significant fact that the elephant was the symbol of President Bush's Republican Party. But unlike the Iraqi leader, the old man told the story with exaggerated gestures, to the sound of giggles from the others in the café. Not a dissident word was expressed, but the message seemed clear: Unless God could come up with magical birds, Iraq had no hope against the allied elephants.

The mood among the soldiers was scarcely more optimistic. In the last days of peace, Saddam visited the trenches in Kuwait and talked to soldiers. They were, plainly, terrified by his presence. The conversations were full of agonizing pauses.

"Where are you from?" he asked one.

"Sulaimaniya, in Kurdistan."

"How are the people in Sulaimaniya?"

"They support you."

A general who later fled to exile in England explained to us that the low morale in the army in Kuwait at the start of the fighting was not because of superior allied weapons. "We knew all about these weapons. We were all circulated with a newsletter about such developments." They simply thought they had been led into an insane enterprise. "We didn't expect a war. We thought it was all a political maneuver."

If Saddam was aware of his subjects' views, he paid little attention. He was under no illusion that they actually liked him. Long before, soon after the 1968 coup that had put his Baath Party in power, Saddam had spoken with a family who had come to complain that one of them had been unjustly executed. "Do not think you will get revenge," he had said then. "If you ever have the chance, by the time you get to us there will not be a sliver of flesh left on our bodies." He meant that there would be too many others waiting in line to tear him and his associates apart.

Since that time, Saddam had eliminated all potential rivals while his host of secret police and intelligence agencies visited immediate and terrible punishment on anyone manifesting, the moment they were detected, the slightest signs of political discontent. He came from Ouija ("the crooked one"), a typical Iraqi village of flat-roofed brick houses, just outside the decayed textile town of Tikrit, perched on the bank of the Tigris a hundred miles north of Baghdad. Even before Saddam, the Tikritis were known for their violence. A British official writing soon after the First World War spoke of "their ancient reputation for savagery and brutality." He favored razing the town to the ground. Saddam's family belonged to the Bejat clan, who were in turn linked to the tribes in and around Tikrit. Their members formed the core of Saddam's regime and consequently expected little mercy if he fell. Tikritis like the Saddam family belonged to the Sunni branch of Islam. Sunnis, who live mostly in the center and north of the country, make up only 20 percent of the total Iraqi population, but they dominated the upper ranks of the army and the administration, as they had since the days when Iraq was part of the Ottoman Empire.

The majority of Iraqis were Shiite Muslims, like the Iranians across the eastern border. Concentrated in Baghdad and on the great flat plain of southern Iraq that stretches all the way to Kuwait and Saudi Arabia, they provided much of the rank and file for the army but were seldom allowed to rise to positions of influence in any Iraqi regime. Since the Baathists had seized control of Iraq, the power of both the political parties they supported and the traditional Shiite tribal sheikhs had been whittled away. If the Shiite showed loyalty to any figures outside the government, it was to their religious leaders. Saddam had instituted a thorough purge of such figures in the early stages of his confrontation with Iran. The survivors had remained quiet.

The Kurds in the mountainous north had always been more of a problem than the Shiites. Non-Arab Sunni Muslims, the Kurds of Iraq, saw themselves as a separate community and had resented rule from Baghdad even in the days when the British held sway there. In the early 1970s, backed by the United States and the shah of Iran, they had launched a fierce insurgency that was defeated only when they were betrayed by their foreign friends. During the Iranian war of the 1980s, some of their leaders had again risen in rebellion and Saddam had retaliated by showering poison gas on Kurdish civilians and by ordering a program of mass executions that killed as many as two hundred thousand Kurds. In addition to this holocaust, the Iraqi leader had wiped four thousand Kurdish villages off the map, herding their inhabitants into cities and refugee camps under the ever-suspicious eyes of his secret police. In the months of crisis that followed Saddam's invasion of Kuwait, the principal Kurdish leaders, Massoud Barzani and Jalal Talabani, seemed to have learned their lesson, pledging neutrality to the Iraqi leader in his confrontation with the allies.

Prior to the invasion of Kuwait and the threat to world oil supplies, Saddam's murderous regime evoked few complaints in the outside world. Even when he took to gassing his Kurdish subjects, governments in Washington, London, and other Western capitals stayed mute, grateful that he was fighting the Islamic Republic of Iran. A strictly enforced rule, laid down after a meeting between Jalal Talabani and a mid-level State Department official in 1988 had drawn an angry protest from Baghdad, forbade any U.S. government official from meeting with any of the exiled Iraqi opposition groups. In 1991, as the United States and other members of the coalition began bombing Iraqi cities, there was no move to rouse the people of Iraq against their dictator. The universal assumption abroad was that in such a viciously efficient police state, where even spilling coffee on the leader's picture in a newspaper could bring swift punishment, there was no prospect of any challenge to the regime from below.

Then, on February 15, a full month into the war, President George Bush suddenly spoke directly to ordinary Iraqis. Twice that day, at the White House and at a missile plant in Massachusetts, he repeated a carefully phrased call for revolt, calling on "the Iraqi military and the Iraqi people to take matters into their own hands and force Saddam Hussein, the dictator, to step aside." The appeal had been conceived of as an incitement to the Iraqi military to stage a coup, and the "Iraqi people" had been included only as an afterthought, but the effects were far-reaching. The president's unequivocal words were broadcast on every international channel that reached Iraq, and millions of Iraqis heard the call. It seemed to them that Bush, Saddam's enemy, whose planes were bombing the country at will, had asked them to join his invincible coalition.

The army in Kuwait, manned largely by Shiite and Kurdish conscripts, was already unwilling to die for Saddam. Once they had realized that the "political maneuver" had failed, they had begun to vote with their feet. Captain Azad Shirwan, an intelligence officer with a tank brigade stationed on the front lines in Kuwait, remembers that by the time the allied ground offensive started on February 24, most of the men in his unit had disappeared. "In our brigade, positions were mostly defended by officers, because the private soldiers had deserted." When Saddam suddenly ordered a general withdrawal from Kuwait the day after the allied ground offensive began, the disintegration became total.

The disappearance of the Iraqi troops bemused the allied generals, who had, in any case, vastly exaggerated the strength of their enemy. "What really amazes me is the lack of bodies," exclaimed General Charles Homer, the U.S. Air Force commander. "There weren't a lot of dead people around. I think a lot of Iraqis just left." Later, the

U.S. government deliberately avoided quantifying the enemy dead for fear that a huge number would serve as useful propaganda for Saddam. In fact, the available evidence suggests that the number of Iraqi casualties was extraordinarily low. "We didn't lose a single officer over the rank of brigadier," says General al-Samarrai, who, as head of military intelligence, was in a position to know.

Casualties among the lower ranks were also light. In one small village, Tulaiha, just off the main road between Baghdad and Kut, 150 men were called up to the army during the Gulf War. Hassan Hamzi, the *mukhtar*, or village leader, insisted that none of them was killed or wounded. The only casualties were two men captured. This compared with thirty dead and eleven prisoners from Tulaiha during the Iran-Iraq war. While Iraq lost 2,100 tanks in Kuwait, U.S. damage-assessment teams found that only 10 percent had been destroyed in battle. The rest had been abandoned.

In the last few days of February, hundreds of thousands of angry soldiers were streaming out of Kuwait, bitter at Saddam Hussein for starting a war they could not win. Hard on the heels of the disappearing enemy, the allied armies swept through Kuwait and across the border into Iraq itself. Saddam thought they might be coming for him. In the final days of the war, he turned up at military intelligence headquarters with his powerful and sinister private secretary, Abed Hamid Mahmoud. "Abed Hamid thinks the allies are coming to Baghdad," he said to General al-Samarrai. "What do you think?" The general disagreed. On February 28, George Bush proved him right by calling a cease-fire; the allied onslaught halted in its tracks. Though his Kuwaiti adventure had turned into a colossal disaster, Saddam now thought the crisis had ended. "After the cease-fire, he thought everything was finished," explains al-Samarrai. It was, in fact, just beginning.

When he first heard the news that Iraqis themselves had risen in revolt, General al-Samarrai was at the emergency headquarters in which he had spent the war, unmolested by the American bombers. The tidings came in a phone call from Basra, far to the south and near the Kuwaiti border. An army general, Hamid Shakar, had been driving to Baghdad with one bodyguard when unknown rebels had attacked and killed him near a paper mill thirty miles north of Basra. Al-Samarrai contacted Saddam, who rushed to the headquarters. He had just arrived, visibly worried, when the phone rang again. Al-Samarrai picked it up and recognized the voice of General Nizar Khazraji, the commander of the entire southwest of the country, with his headquarters in Nassariyah, two hundred miles from Baghdad.

"The rebels are trying to attack us," Khazraji shouted. To convince Baghdad of the seriousness of his situation, he held up the phone, saying, "Don't you hear the sound of the bullets?" The connection was poor and al-Samarrai could hear nothing over the crackling. The besieged commander pleaded for a helicopter to rescue him.

"I told Saddam, who was still sitting in my headquarters, what was happening in Nassariya and he ordered a helicopter to rescue Khazraji," says al-Samarrai. But the army in the south was disintegrating fast. Shiite conscripts were turning on any representative of Saddam's government, including senior officers. The commander of the Iraqi helicopter force said that nothing could be done: "We don't have any helicopters in the area." Soon afterward all contact with the besieged headquarters was lost. Later Saddam and al-Samarrai heard it had been stormed by the rebels and Khazraji severely wounded.

Fanned by the rage of the soldiers streaming out of Kuwait, the revolt spread with the speed of a whirlwind through the cities and towns of the south. Saddam was now staring into the face of disaster.

"We were anxious to withdraw, to end the mad adventure, when Saddam announced withdrawal within twenty-four hours—though without any formal agreement to ensure the safety of the retreating forces," one officer recounted later. "We understood that he wanted the allies to wipe us out: He had already withdrawn the Republican Guard to safety. We had to desert our tanks and vehicles to avoid aerial attacks. We walked a hundred kilometers toward the Iraqi territories, hungry, thirsty, and exhausted." Finally they arrived at the first little town inside their own border. "In Zubair we decided to put an end to Saddam and his regime. We shot at his posters. Hundreds of retreating soldiers came to the city and joined the revolt; by the afternoon, there were thousands of us. Civilians supported us and demonstrations started. We attacked the party building and the security services headquarters."

At 3:00 A.M. on the first of March, the storm reached Basra, the ancient, sprawling city at the junction of the Tigris and Euphrates rivers where in happier days vacationers from teetotal Kuwait had thronged the hotels and nightclubs in search of a bottle of Johnnie Walker Black Label. A single tank gunner expressed his anger at the debacle by firing a round through a portrait of Saddam Hussein, one of the tens of thousands of such pictures that gazed out on every street throughout the country. The soldiers around him applauded his spontaneous act. Within hours, the iron control of Saddam and the Baath Party had been violently cast aside. For the millions of Iraqis who had suddenly found their voices after years of terrified silence, it was the "intifada"—the uprising.

The first that Dr. Walid al-Rawi, the administrator of Basra Teaching Hospital, knew about the uprising was when a policeman visited him to say that incidents were starting in small towns and villages around Basra. "Later that day, a band of fifty rebels came to the hospital and took away three patients who were security men, one of whom they shot on the hospital grounds." As in cities elsewhere in the south, the Baath Party offices were the first to come under attack, Muhammad Kassim, the manager of the Basra Tower Hotel, later told us that on the first day of the uprising, armed men came to his hotel. "They asked if there were any Baathists staying, or any alcohol," he recalled. "I told them no and they went away" The manager of the nearby Sheraton was less persuasive, or perhaps the rebels were less compliant. They set fire to the top stories of the hotel, burning nineteen rooms.

Rampaging through the city, the rebels made a chilling discovery. Beneath the BATA shoe company premises opposite the mayor's office, they found a secret underground prison. Some of the hundreds of prisoners had been shut off from the world so long that they shouted "Down with al-Bakr" as they were released and led into the open air. They believed that the president of Iraq was still Ahmed Hassan al-Bakr, who had been replaced by Saddam Hussein in 1979.

Within days, the intifada had spread to the holy cities of Kerbala, Najaf, and Kufa, the heartland of the Shiite religious tradition to which 55 percent of Iraqis belong. Thirteen hundred years before, the men the Shiite regarded as the Prophet's true heirs, Imam Ali and his sons, Hussein and Abbas, had been martyred here, and their shrines are the focus of adulation from the 130 million devotees of the Shiite faith around the world.

In Najaf, where for a thousand years pilgrims had flocked to the great shrine, its golden dome rising above the low brick houses of the city, the allied bombing had killed thirty-five people. Thirteen members of the al-Habubi family had been crushed by a stick of bombs that had missed a nearby electricity substation and had turned their house into a gray concrete sandwich, the floors collapsing on each other. The rebels said such horrors only underlined the government's inability to protect its people from air attack. At the funeral of a religious notable, Yusuf al-Hakim, on February 14, the crowd chanted against Saddam. By the time the angry rabble of military deserters started straggling into the city in the first two days of March, the government's authority was already fragile.

Brigadier Ali, a professional officer, was among the returning crowd. Born in Najaf, he and many other deserters from the city arrived home on March 2 after being "chased like rats" out of Kuwait. "The streets were full of deserters. All structure in the army was lost. Everybody was their own boss. News was spreading that someone had shot at Saddam's portrait in Basra."

The next day Ali heard there was to be a demonstration in Imam Ali Square, four hundred yards from the great shrine at the center of the city. "At first there were about a hundred people, many of them army officers from Najaf who had deserted. The security forces were well informed and were there as well. The demonstrators started shouting: 'Saddam, keep your hands off. The people of Najaf don't want you.'"

The security men opened fire, further infuriating the demonstrators. Only a few of them were armed, but they threw themselves on the detested but hitherto invulnerable officials. Catching one important local Baath Party functionary, they hacked him to death with knives. Now more people had flooded into the area, drawn by the sound of the shooting. As the security men continued to fire, the demonstrators ran into the warren of alleys and small shops between the square and the shrine. The security forces dashed after them, but the gunfire echoed and reverberated off the walls of the ancient market and they became confused, lost heart, and retreated to their headquarters. It had been no more than twenty minutes or half an hour since the first shouts denouncing Saddam, and the crowd of teenagers and young men in their twenties now controlled the center of the city. Their morale soared.

In a few hours, the newly confident crowd took over the shrine of Imam Ali itself, a golden mosque at the center of a courtyard surrounded by rooms for pilgrims. Unlike the rest of Najaf, the shrine had power from a generator and the demonstrators commandeered its loudspeakers, normally used to call people to prayer, to broadcast simple slogans—"Seek out the criminals"—and urge a final attack on the security forces.

In the evening, the insurgents fought their way into the girls' school used as a local headquarters by the Amn al-Khass, one of the many Iraqi secret police services, and killed eight or nine people there. They were increasingly well armed, having seized submachine guns stockpiled by the government in schools to arm people in case the allies landed from the air. The headquarters of the Quds division of the Republican Guard was just outside the city, but all its combat brigades had been sent to the front and the only garrison consisted of some administrative personnel. These did not resist when officers among the rebels commandeered eighty-two-millimeter mortars and used them to bombard the Baath Party headquarters. "Abdel Amir Jaithoum, my old headmaster, was killed there," recalls Brigadier Ali without regret. "So too was Najim Mizhir, who was the only Baath leader in the city who actually came from Najaf and was quite liked, though he shot a demonstrator." Other Baath Party members fled for their lives through the city's immense cemeteries, filled with the graves of devout Shiite from around the world. By early morning on March 4, the rebels ruled Najaf; within a day, they also held Kerbala, Kufa, and the entire middle Euphrates area.

As Saddam's rule collapsed across southern Iraq, he was assailed by a fresh crisis at his rear. News arrived from the north that the Kurds had also risen.

Unlike the spontaneous and leaderless fury of the southern intifada, the Kurdish revolt was planned. While publicly refusing to take advantage of Saddam's confrontation with the international coalition, the Kurdish leaders had begun planting the seeds of an insurrection well before the end of the war. Massoud Barzani, the small and boyish-faced tribal chief who headed the Kurdistan Democratic Party (the KDP) led by his father years before, had forged an alliance with the other principal commander, Jalal Talahani, the barrel-chested and garrulous leader of the Patriotic Union of Kurdistan (the PUK). They controlled guerrilla forces, turbanned *peshmerga* whose fathers and grandfathers had fought mountain campaigns for half a century against regimes in Baghdad. Before and during the war, agents dispatched by Banani and Talabani had secretly infiltrated the *jash*, a Kurdish militia force recruited by Saddam, in preparation for the moment when their enemy might be weakened enough by the allies for them to strike. As in the country of the Shiite,

George Bush's call to the Iraqi people had resonated with the Kurds, and they had tentatively scheduled the start of their revolt for the middle of March.

The explosion came sooner than that, catching the leadership by surprise. On March 5, in the small mountain town of Rania, police tried to round up some of the army deserters who had arrived home from the debacle in Kuwait. The local *jash*, already suborned by agents of the underground resistance, reacted by seizing control of the town. Within hours the revolt had spread across the sharp crags and winding, narrow canyons of the Kurdish mountains to Sulaimaniya, the provincial capital close to the Iranian border. Here, after two days of hard fighting, the rebels captured the stone fortress that served as the long-dreaded Central Security Headquarters, potent symbol and instrument of the regime. Behind the imposing front entrance, decorated with a giant all-seeing metal eye, they found a medieval warren of torture chambers, equipped with metal hooks, piano wire, and other devices, and smeared with blood. In some rooms, the insurgents discovered freshly strangled women and children. In one, a human ear was nailed to the wall. As in Basra, some of the prisoners had been sealed in underground cells for more than a decade. The outraged crowd fell on the four hundred Baath Party members, intelligence officers, and secret police agents who had holed up in the security headquarters when the revolt began, and massacred them all.

The careful plans of the leadership were swept away as the northern intifada swept across the cities of the mountains and down onto the plains. Two weeks after the first outbreak of rebellion in Rania, the Kurdish *peshmerga* guerrillas captured the vital oil center of Kirkuk, only a few hours' drive from Baghdad. "One second of this day is worth all the wealth in the world," cried an exultant Massoud Barzani. Everywhere people celebrated the man they regarded as their ultimate inspiration with the honorific title "Haji." "Haji Bush," they cried to the few Western correspondents who made their way into liberated Kurdistan at the end of March.

Saddam had now lost control of fourteen of Iraq's eighteen provinces. Baghdad itself remained quiet, but government officials were already showing a readiness to desert the sinking ship. Rumors spread that Saddam had fled the country. In Washington and London, allied officials relaxed in the comforting assumption that no leader could survive such disasters. They were wrong.

The uprisings had taken the rest of the world, as well as Saddam Hussein, completely by surprise. Years before, during the Iran-Iraq war, his exiled opponents had miscalculated the strength of the Iraqi patriotism that he was able to enlist on his side after Iranian forces entered Iraq in 1982. In the crisis after the invasion of Kuwait, exiles made the opposite mistake, underestimating popular anger against Saddam Hussein. When rebellion swept through southern Iraq, the opposition had no organization in the cities capable of directing events. In the town of Hillah, for example, only sixty-six miles from Baghdad, a rebel officer proposed taking the six tanks under his command and leading them to the capital. "The way to Baghdad is open," he cried, but his fellow deserters preferred to concentrate on lynching local Baath officials. In Najaf and elsewhere, euphoria at the overthrow of the regime was followed by anarchy. "At first we were a little crazy," recalls Hameed, a schoolteacher, about these first days in Najaf. "We believed even the traffic lights represented Saddam Hussein, so we wrecked them." Three days after the mob drove out Saddam's forces, there were still dead bodies lying in the streets.

There was only one man in the city with authority, albeit of a spiritual nature. The ninety-one-year-old Grand Ayatollah Abu al-Qassim al-Khoie was the most universally respected cleric in all of Shiite Iraq. He was the grand *Marja* the Shiite equivalent of pope. Born in northwestern Iran, like many other clerics from outside Iraq (Ayatollah Khomeini himself had lived there for sixteen years) he had long lived and taught in Najaf. Unlike Khomeini, al-Khoie was opposed to the Shiite clergy taking power themselves. To the students and disciples gathered around him at the Green Mosque in the great shrine he had always preached that involvement in politics corrupted religion.

On March 6, the frail but venerated grand ayatollah issued a *fatwa*, a religious decree, telling the people: "You are obligated to protect people's property, and honor, likewise, all public institutions, for they are the property of all." He urged the burial of bodies, though without success.

The mood in Najaf was euphoric but confused. "Nobody knew what was going on, but they knew that the city was in our hands," says Sayid Majid al-Khoie, the second son of the grand ayatollah. The night after the rebels took the city he visited the shrine of Imam Hussein and wrote in his diary what the people were saying. "Iraq is finished," said one man, "the Western armies are in Basra and Samawa" (on the Euphrates). Others were saying, "Kerbaja and Najaf are in our hands. Let us go on to Baghdad." People eagerly repeated the rumor that Saddam had left Iraq.

That same day, army officers, encouraged by the ayatollah, formed a committee, but they could not impose discipline on the young men who had led the first demonstrations and now ruled the streets. They could not even take advantage of events that seemed to play into their hands. The commander of the battalion spearheading the government counterattack on Kerbala shot his chief security officer in the head and changed sides. "But the committee could not keep his unit together," laments one of its members. "We had to tell the men to change into their *dishdashah* and go home."

In towns along the Euphrates close to the Iranian border, someone did lay claim to leadership. Muhammad Baqir al-Hakim, the scion of a revered Shiite religious family, had rallied to the Iranian side in the war of the 1980s. Now, from a town just across the border from Basra, he commanded the Supreme Council for the Islamic Revolution in Iraq (SCIRI), and soon, on walls in Basra and in towns, like Amara, close to the border, posters of al-Hakim and the late Iranian leader Ayatollah Khomeini himself began to appear. Announcements in al-Hakim's name claimed full authority over the rebellion: "No action outside this context is allowed; all parties working from Iranian territories should also obey al-Hakim's orders; no party is allowed to recruit volunteers; no ideas except the rightful Islamic ones should be disseminated."

Nothing was more likely to isolate the rebels. The prospect of an Islamic revolution frightened large numbers of Iraqis, such as Sunni Muslims, Kurds, Christians, secular Iraqis, and anyone associated with the Baath Party. Nor were the United States and its allies likely to be reassured by such slogans. So convenient was it for Saddam Hussein for the uprising to be identified with Iran and militant Islam that some Iraqi opposition leaders were quick to believe that he had planted evidence of Iranian involvement. "He sent his own Mukhabarat [secret police] to the south with pictures of Khomeinei," insists Saad Jabr, a veteran of the Iraqi secular opposition. "The Badr Brigade [a pro-Iranian military unit recruited from exiled Iraqis] never came. We talked to the Iranians. They swear by the Koran that they didn't send the pictures."

This denial is echoed by an Islamic Iraqi exile in Iran itself, who exclaims bitterly at the behavior of the Iranians in 1991. "They encouraged the uprising and then betrayed it. They only let a few people cross the border to help, and they would not let them bring arms. They certainly did not put up posters—they were terrified of the American reaction." Whether or not Saddam put up fake posters, he certainly made a crafty effort to publicize the pro-Iranian element in the uprising by releasing eleven members of the al-Hakim family, well known for their alliance to the Tehran regime, in the middle of the crisis. They had been imprisoned in secret for a decade and the outside world had believed them long dead.

Wiser heads among the insurgents in the south knew that everything depended on the Americans. A fatal miscalculation by the U.S. commander in chief, General Norman Schwarzkopf, had allowed the bulk of Saddam's most loyal and proficient military units, the Republican Guards, to escape an allied encirclement twenty-four hours before George Bush called his cease-fire. Unlike the bulk of the Iraqi army, the Republican Guards were not conscript cannon fodder. Schwarzkopf's failure to intercept the guards was to have profound consequences for Iraq. Carefully recruited, well paid, and lavishly equipped, most of them had stayed together while the rest of the army in the south disintegrated. They would be a formidable force against the enthusiastic but chaotic insurgency that had seized control of southern Iraq.

"The biggest reason for the intifada is that they [the rebels] thought the Americans would support them," says Sayid Majid. "They knew they couldn't beat Saddam on their own. They thought they could get control of the cities and that the Americans would stop the army from intervening."

On March 9, Hussein Kamel, Saddam's cousin and son-in-law, began the counterattack on Kerbala, the other great city of Shiite Islam, sixty miles from Najaf. He used

Republican Guard units that had escaped the allied offensive almost intact. Brigadier Ali and other rebel officers went there to help the resistance, but as the Republican Guard tightened its grip around the holy city and terrified civilians fled to nearby villages, he realized that it was the beginning of the end. On the roads out of the city, Iraqi army helicopter crews poured kerosene on the columns of fleeing refugees and then set it alight with tracer fire. American aircraft circled high overhead.

"We had the message that the Americans would support us," lamented the brigadier as he relived his escape back to Najaf from Kerbala in a quiet North London office seven years later. "But I saw with my own eyes the American planes flying over the helicopters. We were expecting them to help; now we could see them witnessing our demise between Najaf and Kerbala. They were taking pictures and they knew exactly what was happening."

Back in Najaf, which itself was about to come under attack, Ali and the other officers consulted with Ayatollah al-Khoie. The venerable Shiite religious leader endorsed the notion that they should go south and contact the allies. "Find out what were their ideas about us, what were they going to do?" He agreed that Sayid Majid should go with them.

As Ali and the little group drove through the towns and villages of anarchic southern Iraq, their car was besieged by crowds who had heard that a son of al-Khoie had come among them. People clamored for arms. The Americans, they said, had stopped the rebels in the river town of Nassariyah taking desperately needed guns and ammunition from the army barracks. In other places, U.S. army units were blowing up captured weapons stores or taking them away. Above all, the rebels wanted communications equipment. Although they had captured almost all of southern Iraq, the successful rebels in individual cities were barely in touch with each other.

Outside Nassariyah, they met their first Americans. They were soldiers manning M-1 Abrams tanks and Bradley armored personnel carriers, part of the huge force that had swept around Kuwait and deep into Iraq in the lightning allied offensive at the end of February. The Iraqis explained to the American commander who they were and why they were there. It was not a warm reception. The U.S. officer went away for ten minutes and then returned with the curious claim that he was out of touch with his headquarters. To a professional military officer like Ali, this seemed highly unlikely. The American curtly suggested that they try and find the French forces, eighty miles to the west.

Bitterly disappointed at this disinterest, the Iraqis went in search of the French. When they eventually found them on March 11, their luck appeared to change. The lieutenant colonel in charge questioned them in detail through an Algerian interpreter and then said he would get in touch with the allied command. He seemed well aware of the significance of the al-Khoie name. Four hours later, he came to report that General Schwarzkopf himself would meet them at Safwan in two days. Safwan was two hundred miles away, too dangerous for a drive across country strewn with Iraqi government units. Could they not use one of the helicopters they could see constantly taking off from the base? asked the little delegation. At first the French told them that a helicopter would be available. For three nights they waited with growing frustration at Samawa, continually being told that the meeting with Schwarzkopf would be delayed. Majid recalls that in conversation the French told them: "The Americans are worried about the Iranians. They asked who brought Khomeini's pictures into Iraq. I explained that I had seen no pictures of Khomeini in any of the cities I had passed through. I said that people were mistaking pictures of my father, Grand Ayatollah al-Khoie, for Khomeini because both were old men with white beards and turbans."

Finally the answer came from the Americans. "We were told they had canceled the meeting in Safwan and that they would not send a helicopter." Majid knew then that the revolt was doomed.

Saddam knew it already. Twelve miles or so north of Baghdad, a heavily guarded compound at al-Rashedia houses the headquarters of the signals intelligence agency that monitored all electronic communications, including calls on satellite phones. Sometime during the first week of the intifada, military intelligence chief Wafiq al-Samarrai was handed a transcript of two radio conversations in southern Iraq that had just been intercepted by one of the al-Rashedia listening posts. Following the procedure for especially urgent intelligence, a copy had already been rushed directly to Saddam.

The intercepted conversations were between two Islamic rebels somewhere near Nassariyah. As recalled by al-Samarrai, they went as follows: "We went to ask the Americans for their support," reported one of the speakers. "They told us, 'We are not going to support you because you are from the al-Sayed group [that would be Muhammad al-Hakim].'"

"Ask them again, go back and ask once more."

The reply soon came. "They say, 'We are not going to support you because you are Shiite and are collaborating with Iran.'"

The American terror over Iranian intervention had condemned the uprising. If the Iraqi leader had indeed organized the distribution of Khomeini's portrait in the insurgent towns, his ruse had succeeded brilliantly. In any event, it was a turning point. Saddam knew he might be saved after all.

"After this message," says al-Samarrai, "the position of the regime immediately became more confident. Now [Saddam] began to attack the intifada."

The first city to fall was Basra, after a mere week outside Saddam's control. In the flatlands of the Mesopotamian plain, which stretches five hundred miles, from the Kurdish mountains to the Gulf, the mechanized forces of the Iraqi army could always outflank and surround the rebels. Iraqi tanks from the Fifty-first Mechanized Division, one of the few units apart from the Republican Guard that escaped mutiny after the Kuwait debacle, quickly captured the main road overlooking the sprawling working-class slums of North Basra. The low brick houses provided little protection against heavy machine gun bullets. The tanks fired shells into centers of resistance like the local fire station, which burned to the ground. "I would say there were more than one thousand dead," said Dr. al-Rawi six weeks later. "Basra General Hospital issued six hundred death certificates. It was a bad time. You could see dogs eating bodies in the streets."

On the mid-Euphrates plain, the fighting was even fiercer. Republican Guard tanks led by Hussein Kamel were first held at al-Aoun, east of Kerbala, but they circled behind the city, cutting it off from the south. To deny the rebels cover for ambushes, the army chopped down or burned palm groves beside the roads. By March 12, says one of those fighting inside the city, "Kerbala was finished, although resistance went on until March sixteenth." Artillery and tank guns systematically blew up the shops and small workshops between the shrines of al-Abbas and al-Hussein, which stand four hundred yards apart. A rocket-propelled grenade hit the blue-and-yellow tiles of the outer porch of the shrine of al-Abbas, the warrior-martyr of Shiite Islam. One memorial of the uprising carefully preserved by the Iraqi troops was a restroom for pilgrims in the al-Abbas shrine, where a noose hung from the ceiling. Here, government officials later explained, pointing to bloodstains on the floor, the rebels hanged or hacked to death Baath Party members.

In every city they captured, the soldiers immediately posted pictures of Saddam Hussein. At the shrine of Imam

Ali in Najaf, where mortar fire had chipped the stones in its courtyard, soldiers placed a strangely inappropriate picture of the Iraqi leader on a chair beside the rubble. He is portrayed dressed in tweeds, walking up an alpine slope, a scene reminiscent of *The Sound of Music.* He smiles as he leans down to pick a mountain flower.

In recaptured cities across southern Iraq, government forces exacted immediate revenge. Grand Ayatollah al-Khoie and his son Muhammad Taqi were taken to Baghdad where, after a night spent in the military intelligence headquarters, they were summoned to a two-hour meeting with an angry Saddam Hussein. As later recalled by Muhammad, who sat silent and let his father do the talking, Saddam said: "I didn't think you would do something like this." The old man replied that he had wanted to control the violence. Saddam replied: "No, you wanted to overthrow me. Now you have lost everything. You did everything the Americans wanted you to do."

While Grand Ayatollah al-Khoie was in Baghdad, some 102 of his students and followers disappeared, never to be seen again. He himself was sent back to a heavily guarded house in Kufa where he remained, lying on a divan, under effective house arrest. Presented by the government to foreign visitors, he would only say ambiguously: "What happened in Najaf and other cities is not allowed and is against God." He told us, "Nobody visits me, so I don't know what is happening. I have trouble with my breathing."

Punishment for involvement in the uprising often took the form of a bullet in the back of the head. But as striking as the atrocities was the casual violence with which Baath Party leaders disposed of suspected enemies. The party always has had a cult of toughness and political machismo, which makes it sometimes record its more violent actions on film to encourage supporters and frighten its enemies.

In March 1991, the party took just such a film of Ali Hassan al-Majid, newly appointed interior minister, cousin of Saddam and known as "Ali Chemical" in Kurdistan for his use of gas against the Kurds in 1988. It showed him and other party leaders hunting down rebels in the fiat and marshy lands around the town of Rumaytha, between the cities of Najaf and Nassariyah in the south.

In the film, al-Majid, who was also briefly governor of Kuwait, shows as little mercy to the Shiite as he did to the Kurds. He tells an Iraqi helicopter pilot on his way to attack rebels holding a bridge: "Don't come back until you are able to tell me you have burnt them; and if you haven't burnt them, don't come back." At one moment he is joined by Muhammad Haman al-Zubeidi, who later became prime minister, his reputation enhanced because of his toughness during the uprising. He kicks and slaps prisoners as they lie on the ground, saying: "Let's execute one so the others will confess." The prisoners, all in civilian clothes, look frightened and resigned. They are silent, except to say softly: "Please don't do this." There is the crackle of machine-gun fire in the background. Al-Majid, who looks a little like Saddam Hussein, chain-smokes as he interrogates prisoners. Of one man he says: "Don't execute this one. He will be useful to us." The soldiers, from an elite unit, shout "Pimp" and "Son of a whore" at another prisoner.

By March 16, Saddam felt confident enough to address his people in a broadcast speech. He explained that he had said nothing immediately after the war, preferring to wait "until tempers had cooled. . . . In addition, recent painful events in the country have kept me from talking to you." He blamed the southern uprising on Iranian agents—"herds of rancorous traitors, infiltrated from inside and outside the country"—while reminding his Kurdish listeners that "every Kurdish movement linked to the foreigner . . . brought only loss and destruction to our Kurdish people," and that neighboring countries would never permit independence for Iraqi Kurds out of fear of their own Kurdish populations, a valid point. He portrayed himself as the one obstacle to Iraq turning into another Lebanon and endangering the ruling Sunni minority.

In any case, the Kurds had far outrun what they could defend. Massoud Barzani and Jalal Talabani had some fifteen thousand *peshmerga* when they started their offensive. They were joined by over a hundred thousand Jash militia belonging to tribes allied to Saddam, as well as the many Kurds who had deserted from the Iraqi army. But the *jash* turned against Saddam primarily because they thought he was going to lose. A few weeks later, as Saddam redirected toward the north the forces that had crushed the south, this looked less certain. The allies were withdrawing, Saddam retained his grip on Baghdad, and he had retaken Basin and Kerbala. The capture of Kirkuk, where the first

Iraqi oil field began production in 1927, helped galvanize the Sunni core of the regime. They were not prepared to cede control of this vital oil region to the Kurds. A few months later, Izzat Ibrabim al-Dhouri, the Iraqi vice president, admitted to a Kurdish delegation that "only when you Kurds took Kirkuk was it possible to mobilize against you." The Kurds were faced with an insoluble military problem: Two of the largest cities they had captured, Kirkuk and Arbil, sit on the plain below the mountains. They are indefensible by guerrillas armed with light weapons to fight tanks backed by artillery. Sulaimaniya and Dohuk, the other Kurdish provincial capitals, are almost equally vulnerable. But these cities are home to most of the 3 million Kurds. The *peshmerga*, even reinforced by the *jash,* could not retreat into the mountains and deep gorges of Kurdistan and abandon their families in the cities. Instead, they had to flee together. Massoud Barzani recalled later that just before the Iraqi counterattack on March 29 he reviewed thousands of Kurdish volunteers near Rawanduz, in the heart of Kurdistan. A few days later, all had disappeared. He was reduced to defending a vital pass near his headquarters at Salahudin with his own bodyguard. For years, a burned-out Iraqi tank marked the spot where they stopped an Iraqi armored column.

Iraqi helicopters threw flour on the retreating Kurds, giving the impression that they were using chemical weapons. The object was to induce panic on a population with bitter memories of Saddam's lavish use of chemicals on them only three years before; it succeeded all too well.

A million Kurds fled into Iran and Turkey.

By the end of March, Saddam Hussein had retaken all of the south. Samarra, the last town under the control of the rebels, fell on March 29. The Republican Guards entered Sulaimaniya, the last city held by the Kurds in the north, on April 2. Saddam had survived the great rebellions, though only by a whisker. He was so short of equipment that the tanks that finally retook Kerbala were old British Chieftains captured from Iran. Ammunition almost ran out. "We had lost two hundred and five million bullets in Kuwait. When we asked the Jordanians for a few million, they refused," recalls Wafiq al-Samarrai. "By the last week of the intifada, the army was down to two hundred and seventy thousand Kalashnikov bullets." That was enough for two days' fighting.

It had been a narrow escape, but now that Saddam had surmounted the immediate threats of the allies and the uprisings, something of the mood of messianic self-confidence with which he had invaded Kuwait eight months before returned. "Things are not so bad," he said to a confidant after the tide had turned. "In the past, our enemies have taken advantage of our mistakes. In future, we will sit back and take advantage of the mistakes made by them."

Saddam seemed to believe that he could now return to something like the status quo of August 1, 1990, the day before the invasion of Kuwait. But his world had changed. The United States and its allies, principally Great Britain, were determined at the very least that Saddam, their erstwhile ally, should never again be in a position to threaten their interests in the Middle East. Prior to August 1990, he had been left to deal as he wished with his own people even as multibillion-dollar oil sales financed his grandiose ambitions. At the end of March 1991, even with the rebellions suppressed, his domain had shriveled. The economic sanctions forbidding the country's vital oil exports as well as all other normal commerce with Iraq had been imposed by the United Nations Security Council on August 6, 1990. Their original purpose had been to force Iraq out of Kuwait. But, even now that Kuwait had been liberated by the allied armies, the sanctions were still in place. If they were not lifted, Saddam's income—and the standard of living of ordinary Iraqis—would be decided at United Nations headquarters in New York and Washington. Iraq would no longer be a fully independent state. For Saddam Hussein to survive under these circumstances, his enemies would have to make a lot of mistakes.

THE CONFLICTS

CHRISTOPHER DICKEY AND EVAN THOMAS

How Saddam Happened

THE LAST TIME Donald Rumsfeld saw Saddam Hussein, he gave him a cordial handshake. The date was almost twenty years ago, December 20, 1983; an official Iraqi television crew recorded the historic moment.

The once and future Defense secretary, at the time a private citizen, had been sent by President Ronald Reagan to Baghdad as a special envoy. Saddam Hussein, armed with a pistol on his hip, seemed "vigorous and confident," according to a now declassified State Department cable obtained by *Newsweek*. Rumsfeld "conveyed the President's greetings and expressed his pleasure at being in Baghdad," wrote the notetaker. Then

CHRISTOPHER DICKEY *is* Newsweek*'s Paris bureau chief and Middle East regional editor.* EVAN THOMAS *has been assistant managing editor at* Newsweek *since 1991. He is the magazine's lead writer on major news stories. This piece appeared in 2002.*

the two men got down to business, talking about the need to improve relations between their two countries.

Rumsfeld is not the first American diplomat to wish for the demise of a former ally. After all, before the cold war, the Soviet Union was America's partner against Hitler in World War II. In the real world, as the saying goes, nations have no permanent friends, just permanent interests. Nonetheless, Rumsfeld's long-ago interlude with Saddam is a reminder that today's friend can be tomorrow's mortal threat. As President George W. Bush and his war cabinet ponder Saddam's successor's regime, they would do well to contemplate how and why the last three presidents allowed the Butcher of Baghdad to stay in power so long.

The history of America's relations with Saddam is one of the sorrier tales in American foreign policy. Time and again, America turned a blind eye to Saddam's predations, saw him as the lesser evil or flinched at the chance to unseat him. No single policymaker or administration deserves blame for creating, or at least tolerating, a monster; many of their decisions seemed reasonable at the time. Even so, there are moments in this clumsy dance with the Devil that make one cringe. It is hard to believe that, during most of the 1980s, America knowingly permitted the Iraq Atomic Energy Commission to import bacterial cultures that might be used to build biological weapons. But it happened.

America's past stumbles, while embarrassing, are not an argument for inaction in the future. Saddam probably is the "grave and gathering danger" described by President Bush in his speech to the United Nations last week. It may also be true that "whoever replaces Saddam is not going to be worse," as a senior administration official put it to *Newsweek*. But the story of how America helped create a Frankenstein monster it now wishes to strangle is sobering. It illustrates the power of wishful thinking, as well as the iron law of unintended consequences.

America did not put Saddam in power. He emerged after two decades of turmoil in the '60s and '70s, as various strongmen tried to gain control of a nation that had been concocted by British imperialists in the 1920s out of three distinct and rival factions, the Sunnis, Shiites, and the Kurds. But during the cold war, America competed with the Soviets for Saddam's attention and welcomed his war with the religious fanatics of Iran. Having cozied up to Saddam, Washington found it hard to break away—even after going to war with him in 1991. Through years of both tacit and overt support, the West helped create the Saddam of today, giving him time to build deadly arsenals and dominate his people. Successive administrations always worried that if Saddam fell, chaos would follow, rippling through the region and possibly igniting another Middle East war. At times it seemed that Washington was transfixed by Saddam.

The Bush administration wants to finally break the spell. If the administration's true believers are right, Baghdad after Saddam falls will look something like Paris after the Germans fled in August 1944. American troops will be cheered as liberators, and democracy will spread forth and push Middle Eastern despotism back into the shadows. Yet if the gloomy predictions of the administration's many critics come true, the Arab street, inflamed by Yankee imperialism, will rise up and replace the shaky but friendly autocrats in the region with Islamic fanatics.

While the Middle East is unlikely to become a democratic nirvana, the worst-case scenarios, always a staple of the press, are probably also wrong or exaggerated. Assuming that a cornered and doomed Saddam does not kill thousands of Americans in some kind of horrific Gotterdmmerung—a scary possibility, one that deeply worries administration officials—the greatest risk of his fall is that one strongman may simply be replaced by another. Saddam's successor may not be a paranoid sadist. But there is no assurance that he will be America's friend or forswear the development of weapons of mass destruction.

American officials have known that Saddam was a psychopath ever since he became the country's de facto ruler in the early 1970s. One of Saddam's early acts after he took the title of president in 1979 was to videotape a session of his party's congress, during which he personally ordered several members executed on the spot. The message, carefully conveyed to the Arab press, was not that these men were executed for plotting against Saddam, but rather for thinking about plotting against him. From the beginning, U.S. officials worried about Saddam's taste for nasty weaponry; indeed, at their meeting in 1983, Rumsfeld warned that Saddam's use of chemical weapons might "inhibit" American assistance. But top officials in the Reagan administration saw Saddam as a useful surrogate. By going to war with Iran, he could bleed the radical mullahs who had seized control of Iran from the pro-American shah. Some Reagan officials even saw Saddam as another Anwar Sadat, capable of making Iraq into a modern secular state, just as Sadat had tried to lift up Egypt before his assassination in 1981.

But Saddam had to be rescued first. The war against Iran was going badly by 1982. Iran's "human wave attacks" threatened to overrun Saddam's armies. Washington decided to give Iraq a helping hand. After Rumsfeld's visit to Baghdad in 1983, U.S. intelligence began supplying the Iraqi dictator with satellite photos showing Iranian deployments. Official documents suggest that America may also have secretly arranged for tanks and other military hardware to be shipped to Iraq in a swap deal—American tanks to Egypt, Egyptian tanks to Iraq. Over the protest of some Pentagon skeptics, the Reagan administration began allowing the Iraqis to buy a wide variety of "dual use" equipment and materials from American suppliers. According to confidential Commerce Department export-control documents obtained by *Newsweek*, the shopping list included a computerized database for Saddam's Interior Ministry (presumably to help keep track of political opponents); helicopters to transport Iraqi officials; television cameras for "video surveillance applications"; chemical-analysis equipment for the Iraq

Atomic Energy Commission (IAEC), and, most unsettling, numerous shipments of "bacteria/fungi/protozoa" to the IAEC. According to former officials, the bacteria cultures could be used to make biological weapons, including anthrax. The State Department also approved the shipment of 1.5 million atropine injectors, for use against the effects of chemical weapons, but the Pentagon blocked the sale. The helicopters, some American officials later surmised, were used to spray poison gas on the Kurds.

The United States almost certainly knew from its own satellite imagery that Saddam was using chemical weapons against Iranian troops. When Saddam bombed Kurdish rebels and civilians with a lethal cocktail of mustard gas, sarin, tabun, and VX in 1988, the Reagan administration first blamed Iran, before acknowledging, under pressure from congressional Democrats, that the culprits were Saddam's own forces. There was only token official protest at the time. Saddam's men were unfazed. An Iraqi audiotape, later captured by the Kurds, records Saddam's cousin Ali Hassan al-Majid (known as Ali Chemical) talking to his fellow officers about gassing the Kurds. "Who is going to say anything?" he asks. "The international community? F—k them!"

The United States was much more concerned with protecting Iraqi oil from attacks by Iran as it was shipped through the Persian Gulf. In 1987, an Iraqi Exocet missile hit an American destroyer, the USS Stark, in the Persian Gulf, killing thirty-seven crewmen. Incredibly, the United States excused Iraq for making an unintentional mistake and instead used the incident to accuse Iran of escalating the war in the gulf. The American tilt to Iraq became more pronounced. U.S. commandos began blowing up Iranian oil platforms and attacking Iranian patrol boats. In 1988, an American warship in the gulf accidentally shot down an Iranian Airbus, killing 290 civilians. Within a few weeks, Iran, exhausted and fearing American intervention, gave up its war with Iraq.

Saddam was feeling cocky. With the support of the West, he had defeated the Islamic revolutionaries in Iran. America favored him as a regional pillar; European and American corporations were vying for contracts with Iraq. He was visited by congressional delegations led by Senators Bob Dole of Kansas and Alan Simpson of Wyoming, who were eager to promote American farm and business interests. But Saddam's megalomania was on the rise, and he overplayed his hand. In 1990, a U.S. Customs sting operation snared several Iraqi agents who were trying to buy electronic equipment used to make triggers for nuclear bombs. Not long after, Saddam gained the world's attention by threatening "to burn Israel to the ground." At the Pentagon, analysts began to warn that Saddam was a growing menace, especially after he tried to buy some American-made high-tech furnaces useful for making nuclear-bomb parts. Yet other officials in Congress and in the Bush administration continued to see him as a useful, if distasteful, regional strongman. The State Department was equivocating with Saddam right up to the moment he invaded Kuwait in August 1990.

Some American diplomats suggest that Saddam might have gotten away with invading Kuwait if he had not been quite so greedy. "If he had pulled back to the Mutla Ridge [overlooking Kuwait City], he'd still be there today," one ex-ambassador told *Newsweek*. And even though President George H. W. Bush compared Saddam to Hitler and sent a half-million-man army to drive him from Kuwait, Washington remained ambivalent about Saddam's fate. It was widely assumed by policymakers that Saddam would collapse after his defeat in Desert Storm, done in by his humiliated officer corps or overthrown by the revolt of a restive minority population. But Washington did not want to push very hard to topple Saddam. The Gulf War, Bush I administration officials pointed out, had been fought to liberate Kuwait, not oust Saddam. "I am certain that had we taken all of Iraq, we would have been like the dinosaur in the tar pit—we would still be there," wrote the American commander in Desert Storm, General Norman Schwarzkopf, in his memoirs. America's allies in the region, most prominently Saudi Arabia, feared that a post-Saddam Iraq would splinter and destabilize the region. The Shiites in the south might bond with their fellow religionists in Iran, strengthening the Shiite mullahs, and threatening the Saudi border. In the north, the Kurds were agitating to break off parts of Iraq and Turkey to create a Kurdistan. So Saddam was allowed to keep his tanks and helicopters—which he used to crush both Shiite and Kurdish rebellions.

The Bush administration played down Saddam's darkness after the Gulf War. Pentagon bureaucrats compiled dossiers to support a war-crimes prosecution of Saddam, especially for his sordid treatment of POWs. They documented police stations and "sports facilities" where Saddam's henchmen used acid baths and electric drills on their victims. One document suggested that torture should be "artistic." But top Defense Department officials stamped the report secret. One Bush administration official subsequently told the *Washington Post*, "Some people were concerned that if we released it during the [1992 presidential] campaign, people would say, 'Why don't you bring this guy to justice?' "(Defense Department aides say politics played no part in the report.)

The Clinton administration was no more aggressive toward Saddam. In 1993, Saddam apparently hired some Kuwaiti liquor smugglers to try to assassinate former president Bush as he took a victory lap through the region. According to one former U.S. ambassador, the new administration was less than eager to see an open-and-shut case against Saddam, for fear that it would demand aggressive retaliation. When American intelligence continued to point to Saddam's role, the Clintonites lobbed a few cruise missiles into Baghdad. The attack reportedly killed one of Saddam's mistresses, but left the dictator defiant.

The American intelligence community, under orders from President Bill Clinton, did mount covert actions aimed at toppling Saddam in the 1990s, but by most accounts they were badly organized and halfhearted. In the north, CIA operatives supported a Kurdish rebellion against Saddam in 1995. According to the CIA's man on the scene, former case officer Robert Baer, Clinton administration officials back in Washington "pulled the plug" on the operation just as it was gathering momentum. The reasons have long remained murky, but according to Baer, Washington was never sure that Saddam's successor would be an improvement, or that Iraq wouldn't simply collapse into chaos. "The question we could never answer," Baer told *Newsweek*, "was, 'After Saddam goes, then what?' " A coup attempt by Iraqi Army officers fizzled the next year. Saddam brutally rolled up the plotters. The CIA operatives pulled out, rescuing everyone they could, and sending them to Guam.

Meanwhile, Saddam was playing cat-and-mouse with weapons of mass destruction. As part of the settlement imposed by America and its allies at the end of the Gulf War, Saddam was supposed to get rid of his existing stockpiles of chem-bio weapons, and to allow in inspectors to make sure none were being hidden or secretly manufactured. The U.N. inspectors did shut down his efforts to build a nuclear weapon. But Saddam continued to secretly work on his germ- and chemical-warfare program. When the inspectors first suspected what Saddam was trying to hide in 1995, Saddam's son-in-law, Hussein Kamel, suddenly fled Iraq to Jordan. Kamel had overseen Saddam's chem-bio program, and his defection forced the revelation of some of the secret locations of Saddam's deadly labs. That evidence is the heart of the "white paper" used last week by President Bush to support his argument that Iraq has been defying U.N. resolutions for the past decade. (Kamel had the bad judgment to return to Iraq, where he was promptly executed, along with various family members.)

By now aware of the scale of Saddam's efforts to deceive, the U.N. arms inspectors were unable to certify that Saddam was no longer making weapons of mass destruction. Without this guarantee, the United Nations was unwilling to lift the economic sanctions imposed after the Gulf War. Saddam continued to play "cheat and retreat" with the inspectors, forcing a showdown in December 1998. The United Nations pulled out its inspectors, and the United States and Britain launched Operation Desert Fox, four days of bombing that was supposed to teach Saddam a lesson and force his compliance.

Saddam thumbed his nose. The United States and its allies, in effect, shrugged and walked away. While the U.N. sanctions regime gradually eroded, allowing Saddam to trade easily on the black market, he was free to brew all the chem-bio weapons he wanted. Making a nuclear weapon is harder, and intelligence officials still believe he is a few years away from even regaining the capacity to manufacture enriched uranium to build his own bomb. If he can steal or buy ready-made fissile material, say from the Russian mafia, he could probably make a nuclear weapon in a matter of months, though it would be so large that delivery would pose a challenge.

As the Bush administration prepares to oust Saddam,

one way or another, senior administration officials are very worried that Saddam will try to use his WMD arsenal. Intelligence experts have warned that Saddam may be "flushing" his small, easy-to-conceal biological agents, trying to get them out of the country before an American invasion. A vial of bugs or toxins that could kill thousands could fit in a suitcase—or a diplomatic pouch. There are any number of grim end-game scenarios. Saddam could try blackmail, threatening to unleash smallpox or some other grotesque virus in an American city if U.S. forces invaded. Or, like a cornered dog, he could lash out in a final spasm of violence, raining chemical weapons down on U.S. troops, handing out his bioweapons to terrorists. "That's the single biggest worry in all this," says a senior administration official. "We are spending a lot of time on this," said another top official.

Some administration critics have said, in effect, let sleeping dogs lie. Don't provoke Saddam by threatening his life; there is no evidence that he has the capability to deliver weapons of mass destruction. Countered White House national-security adviser Condoleezza Rice, "Do we wait until he's better at it?" Several administration officials indicated that an intense effort is underway, covert as well as overt, to warn Saddam's lieutenants to save themselves by breaking from the dictator before it's too late. "Don't be the fool who follows the last order" is the way one senior administration official puts it.

The risk is that some will choose to go down with Saddam, knowing that they stand to be hanged by an angry mob after the dictator falls. It is unclear what kind of justice would follow his fall, aside from summary hangings from the nearest lamppost.

The Bush administration is determined not to "overthrow one strongman only to install another," a senior administration official told *Newsweek*. This official said that the president has made clear that he wants to press for democratic institutions, government accountability and the rule of law in post-Saddam Iraq. But no one really knows how that can be achieved. Bush's advisers are counting on the Iraqis themselves to resist a return to despotism. "People subject to horrible tyranny have strong antibodies to anyone who wants to put them back under tyranny," says a senior administration official. But as another official acknowledged, "a substantial American commitment" to Iraq is inevitable.

At what cost? And who pays? Will other nations chip in money and men? It is not clear how many occupation troops will be required to maintain order, or for how long. Much depends on the manner of Saddam's exit: whether the Iraqis drive him out themselves, or rely heavily on U.S. power. Administration officials shy away from timetables and specifics but say they have to be prepared for all contingencies. "As General Eisenhower said, 'Every plan gets thrown out on the first day of battle. Plans are useless. Planning is everything'," said Vice President Cheney's chief of staff, I. Lewis (Scooter) Libby.

It is far from clear that America will be able to control the next leader of Iraq, even if he is not as diabolical as

Saddam. Any leader of Iraq will look around him and see that Israel and Pakistan have nuclear weapons and that Iran may soon. Just as England and France opted to build their own bombs in the cold war, and not depend on the U.S. nuclear umbrella, the next president of Iraq may want to have his own bomb. "He may want to, but he can't be allowed to," says a Bush official. But what is to guarantee that a newly rich Iraqi strongman won't buy one with his nation's vast oil wealth? In some ways, Iraq is to the Middle East as Germany was to Europe in the twentieth century, too large, too militaristic, and too competent to coexist peaceably with neighbors. It took two world wars and millions of lives to solve "the German problem." Getting rid of Saddam may be essential to creating a stable, democratic Iraq. But it may be only a first step on a long and dangerous march.

MICAH L. SIFRY

America, Oil, and Intervention

WHY IS THE UNITED STATES in the Persian Gulf? "What is at stake is far more than a matter of economics or oil," President Bush insists. "What is at stake is whether the nations of the world can take a common stand against aggression . . . whether we live in a world governed by the rule of law or by the law of the jungle." We will probably not learn the real reasons for this intervention for years, until some future Daniel Ellsberg comes forward or when the classified documents and cables revealing the administration's thinking are released.

MICAH L. SIFRY *is senior analyst with Public Campaign and a frequent contributor to* Salon *and* Mother Jones *magazine. He is the editor of the* Gulf War Reader *and author of* Spoiling for a Fight: Third-Party Politics in America. *This piece was written 1999.*

But this isn't the first time the United States moved thousands of troops and the machines of war into the Middle East in response to events in Iraq. Nor is this the first time national security planners contemplated using force to defend Kuwait. In the summer of 1958 they did both of those things. At that time, the deployment of fourteen-thousand troops to Lebanon to shore up its pro-Western government was viewed as another episode in the ongoing cold war; the operation was triggered by an anti-Western coup in Iraq and supposedly focused on blocking Communist designs on Lebanon. But as recently released high-level documents show, the United States intervention had no more to do with the rights of small nations, opposition to aggression, dictators on the loose, or a new world order than we suspect it does now.

On July 14, 1958, a group of Communists, nationalists, and Nasserists overthrew the British-installed Iraqi regime of Premier Nuri as Said, setting off tremors throughout the region and calls for assistance from the pro-Western governments of Lebanon and Jordan. In the *New York Times,* Iraq was described as an "irreplaceable source of oil," the "keystone of the Baghdad Pact" (a British-inspired alliance of Turkey, Pakistan, Iraq, Iran, and Britain) and "the last bastion of Western influence" in the region. Indeed, Said had been an eager and active participant in a covert British-American effort to depose the left-leaning government of Syria that had been foiled the year before. The coup was deemed a "severe blow" to U.S. prestige, and it was assumed that Nasser or the Russians, or both, were behind it. Furthermore, it was reported that the British were worried about "the possibility of a coup in the oil-rich Sheikdom of Kuwait" and were discussing "armed intervention in Iraq." How did the United States react?

When news of the takeover reached Washington on the morning of the 14th, a group led by Secretary of State John Foster Dulles, General Nathan Twining, Chair of the Joint Chiefs of Staff, and Director of Central Intelligence Allen Dulles met at the State Department to discuss their options before briefing President Eisenhower. According to a Memorandum for the Record titled "Meeting re Iraq," the group agreed that if the United States did nothing

> 1. Nasser would take over the whole area;
>
> 2. the United States would lose influence not only in the Arab States of the Middle East but in the area generally, and our bases throughout the area would be in jeopardy;
>
> 3. the dependability of United States commitments for assistance in the event of need would be brought into question throughout the world.

The memo continues, "General Twining felt that in these circumstances we had no alternative but to go in." The rest of that paragraph was deleted, but according to William Quandt, a senior staff member of the National Security Council in the 1970s who has written a careful analysis of the Lebanon episode in Force Without War, Twining had proposed an "area-wide counteroffensive" that would have sent the United States into Lebanon, Britain into Iraq and Kuwait, Israel into the West Bank of Jordan, and Turkey into Syria. The memo further reports that "Mr. [Donald] Quarles [Acting Secretary of Defense] attached great importance to having a United Nations or other |umbrella' under which to operate so as to give adequate moral sanction to our action." And it concludes with the assessment that "intervention involves the risk of general war" with the Soviet Union, but that "we should face the risk now as well as any time."

Fortunately, Eisenhower did not rush to embrace General Twining's proposal, even though British Prime Minister Harold MacMillan was urging similar action. Fears of a pro-Nasser wave sweeping the region were certainly real among the Western leaders. Aside from the loss of bases and credibility, the West stood to lose control over some very important oil concessions. And access to oil was the crucial factor in deciding the course of both world wars. In 1958 Kuwait was the leading Middle East oil producer, at about 1.15 million barrels a day (mbd). There the concession was shared equally by British Petroleum and Gulf Oil. Saudi Arabian oil, pumped by the Arab American Oil Company (Aramco), a consortium of four American oil companies, accounted for another 1 mbd. An international group divided Iran's output of .85 mbd. In Iraq the British and French governments both owned close to one-quarter of the Iraq Petroleum Corporation, which produced .7 mbd. At the time, oil companies shared their profits on a fifty-fifty basis with their host governments. The $200 million that Iraq received from the I.P.C. amounted to half its annual revenues. Indeed, popular resentment against Britain's exploitation of Iraq's resources fueled the coup against Said's regime.

When Eisenhower met with his advisers at noon on the 14th, his first concern was how to respond to an urgent plea from Camille Chamoun, the Christian President of Lebanon—though the Persian Gulf was very much on his mind, as we shall see. Early in 1957, the United States had announced that it would defend any country in the Middle East "requesting assistance against armed aggression from any country controlled by international communism," a step it took to counter potential radical gains in the wake of the British-French reversal the United States had engineered at Suez the year before. Chamoun had been the only Middle Eastern leader to endorse what became known as the Eisenhower Doctrine, and he had been quietly calling for help for months. Ever since Chamoun had won an overwhelming victory in the 1957 Lebanese legislative elections—thanks in good part to suitcases of money delivered by C.I.A. operative Wilbur Crane Eveland—he had been under attack by Muslim and Druse leaders for having tipped Lebanon too far to the West. In the spring of 1958, this dissent began to spill into the streets, in a dress rehearsal for the civil war that tore Lebanon apart seventeen years later. Even before the July 14 coup in Iraq, Eisenhower had been inclined to move into Lebanon to show U.S. resolve, despite the lack of evidence of international Communist subversion. Now, as he wrote in his memoir, *Waging Peace*, "the time had come to act."

There were two prongs to Eisenhower's intervention: the very public landing of fourteen-thousand troops to defend the "integrity and independence" of a small nation, Lebanon, in tandem with a British deployment of several thousand troops into Jordan, and some serious saber rattling in the Persian Gulf to impress the Iraqis, Russians, and Egyptians, as well as the British, that the United States meant business.

In his message to Congress, Eisenhower justified the U.S. action by claiming the "events in Iraq demonstrate a ruthlessness of aggressive purpose which tiny Lebanon cannot combat without further evidence of support from friendly nations." At the United Nations, U.S. ambassador Henry Cabot Lodge declared the Lebanon was the victim of "indirect aggression," and he drew parallels to Italy's invasion of Ethiopia, Germany's annexation of Austria, and the Communist takeover of Czechoslovakia. As Quandt puts it, "Nothing was said of broad concerns with Iraq, oil, or the Arab-Israeli conflict. For the public purposes this was a Lebanese crisis, behind which communism's malign influence could be detected." The Soviet Union and the nonaligned countries were quick to condemn the American and British moves as Western imperialism, and a banner headline in the *New York Times* ominously reported, "Soviet Charges Move Threatens New War."

Until the makeup and intentions of the new Republic of Iraq became clear, "general war" was a real possibility. Eisenhower ordered a worldwide military alert of U.S. forces and the Strategic Air Command, the Times reported that an "atomic until" based in Germany had been dispatched to Lebanon, and the Russians began large-scale maneuvers along their border with Turkey and Iran. Historians disagree on whether the Lebanon and Jordan deployments were intended to give the West the ability to take further action in Iraq or in the Persian Gulf. While Quandt argues that the intervention was always meant to be a limited one, Harvard scholar Nadav Safran writes in *Saudi Arabia: The Ceaseless Quest for Security* that the troops were moved "to be in a position to intervene in Iraq if the opportunity arose."

Certainly, Iraq's threat to the oil-rich sheikdoms of the gulf was taken very seriously. On the first day of the crisis, Eisenhower ordered a Marine Corps regimental combat team based in Okinawa to the gulf "to guard against a possible Iraqi move into Kuwait," he writes in *Waging Peace.* In addition, he recalls, "I instructed General Twining to be prepared to employ, subject to my personal approval, whatever means might become necessary to prevent any unfriendly forces from moving into Kuwait." According to Quandt, who interviewed several of the American principals, "It seems clear that Eisenhower was referring to the possible use of nuclear weapons, an issue that was discussed several times during the crisis."

Newly uncovered documents from the British Public Record Office and the N.S.C. give undeniable evidence of what was behind the British and American actions. Here is an excerpt from a July 19, 1958, cable sent by Foreign Secretary Selwyn Lloyd from the British Embassy in Washington back to London:

> They [the U.S. government] are assuming that we will take firm action to maintain our position in

Kuwait. They themselves are disposed to act with similar resolution in relations to the Aramco oilfields in the area of Dahran. . . . They assume that we will also hold Bahrain and Qatar, come what may.

They agree that at all costs these oilfields must be kept in Western hands.

In an undated but contemporaneous N.S.C. report on "Issues Arising Out of the Situation in the Near East," American security planners carefully assessed the pros and cons of military action:

Should the United States be prepared to support, or if necessary assist, the British in using force to retain control of Kuwait and the Persian Gulf?

1. The argument for such action: An assured source of oil is essential to the continued economic viability of Western Europe. . . . If Nasser obtains dominant influence over the Persian Gulf-oil producing areas, Western access to this oil might be seriously threatened. The only way to guarantee continued access to Persian Gulf oil on acceptable terms is to insist on maintaining the current concessions.

2. The argument against such action: If armed force must be used to help retain this area (or even if there is a public indication of willingness to use force), the benefits of any actions in the direction of accommodation with radical Pan-Arab nationalism will be largely lost and U.S. relations with neutral countries elsewhere would be adversely affected. Such accommodation would better provide the

> basis for continued assurance of access of Kuwait and Persian Gulf oil.

Note the focus on quelling or controlling the forces of Arab nationalism, and the absence of the Soviet bogeyman. At that stage of the cold war, the United States had an overwhelming edge over the Soviet Union. For all his threatening bluster, Soviet leader Nikita Khrushchev had done little to help Egypt during the Suez crisis. Apparently Eisenhower understood that, and after some angry speeches at the U.N., the superpower confrontation generated by the Lebanon deployment rapidly cooled down.

The Iraqis also understood, then, the limits of their revolution. On July 18, 1958, a *Times* headline announced, "West to Keep Out of Iraq Unless Oil Is Threatened." Eisenhower and Lloyd had met and, as Dana Adams Schmidt reported in the paper of record, decided that "for the time being . . . intervention will not be extended to Iraq as long as the revolutionary government in Iraq respects Western oil interests." Dutifully, later that day Baghdad Radio announced Iraq's intentions to "respect its obligations." Once the feared move on the West's oil was averted, the supposed threat to the Chamoun government shrank in importance. Eisenhower sent Robert Murphy, a career diplomat, to Beirut, where he "quickly concluded that Communism had nothing to do with the crisis is Lebanon," writes Quandt. A successor to Chamoun acceptable to all sides was found in the person of General Fuad Chehab, head of the Lebanese Army. Ironically, in a communication to the U.S. government months earlier, Nasser had proposed precisely this solution to Lebanon's internal political crisis.

Thus what followed the coup in Iraq and the landing of troops in Beirut was a new understanding of the rules of the Middle East game: Political changes were possible as long as economic interests were safeguarded. And the United States—not Great Britain—would decide which moves were acceptable and which should be blocked. An N.S.C. report dated November 4, 1958, neatly encapsulates official thinking on the region:

> Be prepared, when required, to come forward with formulas designed to reconcile vital Free World interests in the area's petroleum resources with the rising tide of nationalism in the area. . . . Be prepared to use force, but only as a last resort sort . . . to insure that the quantity of oil available from the Near East on reasonable terms is sufficient, together with oil from other sources, to meet Western Europe's requirements, recognizing that this course will cut across the courses of action envisioned above toward Arab nationalism and could not be indefinitely pursued.

In a parenthetical remark buried in a footnote, our anonymous N.S.C. planner adds that a study was being done on the "feasibility over the longer term" of reducing the "dependence" of the West of Middle Eastern oil.

In the thirty-three years since this episode, the United

States has tried a variety of "formulas" aimed at protecting its interests in the region while "accommodating" Arab nationalism. The leaders of Jordan, Egypt, Morocco, and Lebanon have been protected (and spied upon) by C.I.A.-trained security units, as Bob Woodward revealed in *Veil;* for twenty years Jordan's King Hussein even received annual stipends from the agency. Surrogates for U.S. power, like the Shah of Iran and the Israelis, have been armed and given broad latitude, and everybody else with money—regardless of his despotic ways—was sold weapons as well. A peace agreement that removed the major threat of another Arab-Israeli war was brokered between Egypt and Israel, but only at the expense of the indefinite deferral of Palestinian aspirations.

For a good part of the 1980s, Saddam Hussein was seen as "our" strongman and functioned as such in fighting the Ayatollah. Presumably, had Saddam done as expected and taken only a nibble out of Kuwait, the United States would now merely be bolstering Saudi Arabia as its latest surrogate. But the seizure of Kuwait was a bold and un-deniable affront to America's domain. It shouldn't seem strange to hear once again the claim of protecting small nations from aggression as a justification for American intervention, or to find a "Nazi" threat invoked in the absence of the Russian bear. The sad fact is that instead of ending America's dependence on oil and encouraging democratic movements for self-determination across the Middle East, Washington has simply relied on one unstable formula after another to maintain its dominance. Now it's all blowing up in our face.

EFRAIM KARSH

Politics Is a Lethal Game

THIRTY-FOUR YEARS AGO, Nikita Khrushchev made his famous speech at the Twentieth Congress of the Soviet Communist Party, revealing for the first time the full scope of Stalin's atrocities. As he spoke, one story goes, a note was passed forward from the audience. Khrushchev unfolded the piece of paper, glanced at it briefly, and read it aloud: "'If Stalin was such a monster, why didn't you and the rest of the Soviet leadership stand up to him?'" "This is an excellent question," said Khrushchev. "I would be grateful if the comrade who asked it would rise so that I can answer him face to face." Nobody moved. "Well,' said the Soviet leader, "there's the answer to your question."

EFRAIM KARSH *is professor and head of the Mediterranean Studies Program at King's College, University of London. He is the author of numerous books such as* Empires of the Sand, *and* Saddam Hussein, A Political Biography. *This piece is from 1990.*

Such is the logic of dictatorship, and little has changed since Khrushchev deftly made his point. Substitute Baghdad for Moscow, and the scene might very well be repeated when future Iraqi leaders meet to assess the Saddam Hussein era. For during his twenty-one years in power—a decade as de facto leader under President Ahmed Hassan al-Bakr and eleven years in the top spot—the fifty-three-year-old dictator has fully subordinated Iraq's political system to his will, sterilized its government institutions, and reduced the national decision-making apparatus to one man, surrounded by a docile flock of advisers and ministers.

The transformation did not take place overnight. Since 1963, Iraq has been ruled by the Baath Party, whose ideology is a mixture of socialism and pan-Arabism. Secular, modernizing, but anti-Western, the Baath Party in theory pursues the grand design of forging the Arab states into a single nation. But the nation states of the Middle East have proven more enduring than the mirage of Arab unity. The Baathists have therefore concentrated on achieving absolute control over Iraq's state institutions.

The foremost decision-making body in Iraq is the Revolutionary Command Council, defined by the Iraqi Constitution as "the supreme legislative and executive authority in the state." Its chairman is also the President of the state, Secretary General of the Baath Party, and the Commander in Chief of the Armed Forces. Second to the council in political importance is the Regional Command of the Baath, the party executive. Third is the Council of Ministers.

Until the late 1970's, no single person or faction

dominated these institutions. They functioned as genuine collective decision-making bodies, and were often the arena for heated debates. Saddam Hussein, however, did not flinch before the challenge of eliminating these manifestations of pluralism. In the late 1960s, as Iraq's young and ambitious vice president, he began purging actual and potential rivals in the Revolutionary Command Council and the Regional Command. A decade later, he took up residence in the presidential palace.

But a tyrant's work is never done. His is a constant struggle for personal survival. If there is one lesson to be learned from the violent end of dictators, from Nero to the Iraqi despot Abdel Karim Kassem, killed in a coup in 1963, it is that holding on to power can often be as demanding as seizing it.

Hussein is no historian, but this lesson has never been lost on him. Immediately after becoming president in 1979, he launched his most brutal, far-reaching purge yet. Dozens of military officers and party officials, including five of the Revolutionary Command Council's twenty-two members, were accused of taking part in a Syrian plot against the regime, given summary trials, and executed. Hussein videotaped his public "exposure" of key "traitors" at a large gathering of party officials. Cassettes, distributed to senior officials of other Arab countries, show Hussein reading off the names of the supposed traitors, slowly and theatrically, pausing occasionally to light his cigar. Everyone in the audience sweats, as those on the list are led away, one by one.

Once he had reduced Iraq's governing institutions to rubber stamps, Hussein filled key posts with longtime party associates and family members, as well as more distant relatives and neighbor from his hometown. Today he rules Iraq through this small clique.

The rules of the game for Hussein's coterie are simple and straightforward: they give their ruler unconditional loyalty and obedience in return for important political posts. But the footing at the top of the pyramid is treacherous. Should a member of the inner circle find his loyalty called into question, or should it become too popular, his political career will quickly go into decline, whatever his former standing.

Take the case of Adnan Khairallah Talfah, the Iraqi Minister of Defense, who died mysteriously in a helicopter crash in May 1959. The official explanation was that the helicopter had flown into a sandstorm. Few believed this. Too many senior military officials had met their end in similar accidents following the Iran-Iraq war. Even the most trusting Iraqis found it difficult to comprehend why they seemed to be losing more helicopters in peacetime than at the height of the war.

Even in a regime that thrives on purges, Adnan Khairallah's case was remarkable, for he and Hussein were bound by ties of kinship and affection. Hussein's father, a landless peasant in the small northern town of Tikrit, died before his son was born, and the boy spent most of his childhood with the family of Khairallah Talfah, his maternal uncle and Adnan's father.

After Hussein's strong-willed mother, Khairallah, an army officer and ardent Arab nationalist, probably had the most influence on melding the future leader's personality. By Hussein's own account, it was Khairallah who fueled his hatred of the old regime and colonialism (Khairallah's military career was ruined when he took part in Prime Minister Rashid Ali's ill-fated 1941 uprising, intended to drive the British from Iraq). Emulating his uncle, Hussein applied for entry to the prestigious Baghdad Military Academy, but failed the entrance examination. He later married Khairallah's daughter, Sajida.

Throughout childhood, Hussein enjoyed an unusually close relationship with Adnan. It was a seven-year-old Adnan who, in 1947, convinced his illiterate cousin, then ten years old, to defy his family, leave his village and seek education in Tikrit. Friendship was rewarded. Though a lackluster officer with no national standing, in 1977 Staff Colonel Adnan Khairallah became one of the few military representatives on the Revolutionary Command Council and the Regional Command. Any doubt about who had pulled the strings behind this promotion were completely dispelled two years later when Hussein, now president, appointed Khairallah Minister of Defense, Deputy Prime Minister, and Deputy Commander in Chief of the Armed Forces. Khairallah repaid his benefactor by ensuring the absolute loyalty of the armed forces through systematic purges, and by serving as Hussein's right hand during the eight years of war against Iran.

Yet none of this mattered once Khairallah sided with

his sister in a family feud over Hussein's romantic involvement with Samira Shahbandar, ex-wife of the chairman of Iraqi Airways and a member of a respected Baghdad family. Unlike previous presidential romances, which had carefully been kept secret, Hussein's affair with Shahbandar became public knowledge, rocking his marriage and damaging the president's carefully nurtured image as a faithful husband and devoted family man.

To make matters worse, Hussein's eldest son, Uday, decided to avenge his mother's honor by publicly clubbing to death the presidential food taster, who happened to perform services in addition to his gastronomical responsibilities. It was he who had introduced Shahbandar to Hussein and had served as a go-between for the two lovers. Furious, Hussein put his son behind bars and pledged to try him on murder charges, but after a highly emotional campaign by his wife and Adnan Khairallah, he relented and sent Uday into luxurious exile in Switzerland.

Although relations within the presidential family eventually thawed (Uday was allowed to return to Baghdad in the spring of 1990), Hussein did not forgive Khairallah for his involvement in the affair, which embarrassed him before the public. A few months after the scandal, he ferociously attacked the Minister of Defense, accusing him of failing to respond effectively to a coup attempt in early 1989. The handwriting was on the wall.

In truth, Khairallah was already a marked man. He had made the serious mistake of sharing glory for the "victory over the Persian enemy" with Saddam Hussein. For this sin, there could be no absolution, as any number of prominent generals were also to find out. Maher Abdel Rashid and Hisham Sabah al-Fakhri, national heroes after liberating the Fao Peninsula from Iranian occupation in April 1988, were relieved of their commands later that year and today are believed to be under house arrest. Rashid's mistake was to grant a few interviews to the Kuwaiti press that temporarily put him in the spotlight.

Khairallah's unhappy fate was atypical for members of Hussein's entourage who have lost favor. Although Hussein relied heavily on executions when purging the various state organs, he has tended to deal more gently with close associates. Disgraced dependents have usually been shunted to lesser positions and allowed to slide gracefully into obscurity. After Naim Haddad, a prominent Shiite in Hussein's administration, was implicated in a 1986 coup attempt and disappeared from the political scene, he was allowed to return to his home village. Hussein's half-brother Barzan Ibrahim al-Tikriti (after her husband's death, his mother married her brother-in-law. Ibrahim Hassan) was removed as head of the intelligence services in 1983 but was brought in from the cold six years later and appointed Ambassador to the United Nations in Geneva. At the same time, another half-brother, Watban Ibrahim al-Tikriti, who had been demoted with Barzan in 1983, was made head of public security. All told, surprisingly few of Hussein's inner circle have fallen into disrepute during the past two decades, suggesting that even in a system permeated by distrust and betrayal, a feeling of solidarity is not unknown.

This solidarity does not rest entirely on the nobler emotions. In his gradual rise to absolute power, Hussein has managed to tie his inner circle to his policies and, consequently, to his own fate. Many of them have played a highly visible rote in the purges (Naim Haddad, for example, headed the special tribunal that ordered the notorious executions of 1979); some, it has been rumored, have picked up a rifle and joined Hussein on firing squads.

The links binding Iraq's ruling clique to Hussein were further tempered during the Iran-Iraq war. Aware that they, too, and not only their autocrat, had been singled out as enemies by the clerics in Teheran, and well aware of the merciless retribution meted out by Hussein for indecisiveness in those fateful days, the inner circle rallied more closely than ever around the only person who, in their view, could save the day.

No one knew better than Tariq Aziz, Hussein's closest adviser on foreign affairs, the dire consequences an Iranian victory would mean for him and his associates. In April 1980, he narrowly escaped an assassination attempt by Al Dawa, the pro-Iranian Shiite underground organization. The gray-haired, soft-spoken politician, who since 1983 has held the post of Foreign Minister in addition to that of Deputy Prime Minister, is widely regarded as the moderate face of the regime. His primary task—to justify Iraqi policies to the world—has nevertheless become increasingly difficult of late, with the execution of the British journalist Farzad Bazoft in March and the recent occupation of Kuwait. A Christian in a Muslim administration, he is entirety a creature of Hussein, attending carefully to his master's voice.

Aziz's predecessor in the Foreign Ministry, Saadun Hammadi, is also a member of the circle. A sixty-year-old Shiite who has devotedly backed Hussein since the early 1970s, Hammadi resigned from the Foreign Ministry in 1983 for health reasons, only to become a trusted adviser on economic affairs and, in this capacity, one of the few men to whom Hussein listens.

While Aziz and Hammadi speak softly for the regime, Taha Yasin Ramadan carries the big stick. Commander of the Popular Army, Iraq's praetorian militia, for the past two decades, Ramadan is a miniature version of Hussein, well-practiced in anti-Western, nationalistic rhetoric and, unusual among those surrounding Hussein, endowed with personal charisma. This quality has enabled him to build up a power base that, according to observers outside Iraq, might well make him a contender for the country's leadership.

So far, Ramadan has given no indication that he entertains any such thought. Rather, he has used his power to enforce the president's will. Yet Hussein has always taken care to keep Ramadan on a short leash, in the past using Khairallah as counterweight; more recently, rumor has it that his power is waning.

Hussein's personal experience has also led him to deal cautiously with his official No. 2., Izzat Ibrahim. Bearing in mind his own success in using the deputy chairmanship of the Revolutionary Command Council as a springboard to absolute power, Hussein has kept his deputy a ceremonial figure, denying him any real hold on the levers of power. Unlike Hussein, whose portrait appears on every corner, Izzat Ibrahim remains an anonymous figure; rarely do his subordinates see him on television, hear him on the radio, or read his speeches in the press. To reinforce Ibrahim's loyalty, Hussein arranged for Ibrahim's daughter to marry his eldest son, Uday. Ibrahim's failing health also makes him an unlikely challenger to Hussein's power. Ibrahim's main asset for Hussein is his religious piety, which has made him the Baath's main negotiator with Iraq's Shiite clergy.

Also tied to Hussein by marital bonds is the young and energetic Minister of Industry and Military Production, General Hussein Kamel. A cousin and a son-in-law of Hussein, Kamel is regarded by many as a rising star. The best indication of Kamel's growing prominence is his responsibility for developing Iraq's nonconventional arms industry, including the nuclear project, on which Hussein has pinned hopes for regional hegemony. Kamel also commands the country's long-range missile units, which will be crucial if fighting breaks out in the Gulf.

Kamel may even be more influential than the present Minister of Defense, Abdel Jabbar Khalil Shanshal. An elderly professional soldier, Shanshal has the virtue, from a presidential point of view, of having no experience or interest in politics (he is probably not even a member of the Baath Party). By moving Shanshal into Khairallah's vacant position, Hussein apparently hoped to kill two birds with one stone: to eliminate mutterings in the military regarding the premature death of the Minister of

Defense and to ensure that a docile figure occupied a potentially influential post.

Hussein's closest dependents have always staked their political future, indeed their lives, on the success of his policies, while exercising virtually no influence on his major decisions. Should Hussein be deposed, they will most likely go down with him; should they overachieve in his service, he will reap the fruits of their labors, while they will be left to count their blessings at not being purged for their successes. At most, Hussein's inner circle has served as an echo chamber, amplifying his wishful thinking and backing those political options they believe he is inclined to adopt. As with other megalomanical leaders like Nicolae Ceausescu of Romania and the Shah of Iran, who were told only what they wanted to hear, Hussein's judgment of the real world has been fundamentally distorted by the Byzantine atmosphere of flattery and self-abasement that surrounds him.

The autocrat, whose only contact with his subjects amounts to glances from behind the tinted windows of a speeding limousine, carefully staged photo opportunities, or speeches made at heavily guarded rallies, is convinced of the love and admiration of his people. He was reported to have boasted that were he to sell pebbles in the streets of Baghdad, people would be willing to buy them for a fortune, for in his hands, they would be seen as pearls.

Hussein's growing isolation from the real world has so far resulted in two major miscalculations: the invasion of Iran in September 1980 and the occupation of Kuwait a decade later.

Police states do not make a habit of divulging information about their decision-making process. Evidence of what actually happens in the dark corridors of power must be gathered from second- and third-hand sources. Often it is flimsy. However, as far as it can be ascertained, no one in Iraq's political leadership contested Hussein's decision to take on the aged Ayatollah Khomeni. Rather, the inner circle rallied sheeplike around their leader during the tense year preceding the war. When Hussein hoped to contain the Iranian threat without going to war, his associates backed him whole-heartedly; once he had made up his mind to resort to arms, they quickly forgot their previous moderation and insisted on the advantages of invading Iran.

Nor is there evidence that any serious planning took place before the invasion of Kuwait. Had Hussein followed the inclination of his main foreign-policy advisers—Tariq Aziz and his Deputy Foreign Minister, Nizar Hamdoon—the invasion might not have occurred. At most, Kuwait might have been forced to meet the growing financial demands of its big brother to the north. But these two experts on foreign affairs apparently remained mute.

Hussein probably swayed his associates by insisting that the occupation of Kuwait would be a swift and costless march, nothing like the war against Iran. The Arab world would applaud Iraq's resolve to redistribute the wealth of the corrupt Kuwaitis among the poorer Arab masses. Resistance from the West would amount to feeble mutterings. After all, hadn't Iraq publicly humiliated Great Britain by executing the "spy" Farzad Bazoft?

Aziz and Hamdoon's reluctance to express any reservations is understandable. Hussein does not lake criticism well. One of the better-known stories illustrating his attitude toward free debate concerns a Cabinet meeting held in the summer of 1982. In those dark, hopeless days, when Baghdad was bracing for an Iranian invasion, the Minister of Health, Riyadh Ibrahim, suggested that Hussein step dawn temporarily in order to pave the way far a negotiated cease-fire. The Iraqi president, the story goes, showed no sign of irritation at this heretical idea. "Let us go to the other room and discuss the matter further," he suggested. The minister agreed, and the two left the room. A moment later, a shot was heard, and Hussein returned alone to the Cabinet as though nothing had happened. The question of his resignation did not come up again.

Whether or not this incident actually task place—the government claimed that the Minister had been executed for distributing tainted medicine—the often-repeated story reflects the deep fear that grips Hussein's inner circle, which in turn raises serious doubts about the ability of the Iraqi political elite to stand up to him. Among the country's institutions, only the military could seriously challenge Hussein. But how willing and well prepared would it be for the task? Its conduct during the Iran-Iraq war provides a number of clues.

In nondemocratic systems, force is the main agent of political change. Hussein knows this only too well, and he has spared no effort to transform the military into an "ideological force" loyal only to him. Scores of party commissars have been deployed throughout the armed forces, right down to the battalion level. Organized political activity has been banned; "unreliable" elements have been purged and often executed. The social composition of the Republican Guard, an elite corps within the army, has been fundamentally transformed, so that now it draws heavily on conscripts from Tikrit and the surrounding region.

To win over the military, Hussein has improved its standard of living and has tried to convince the officer corps that he is one of them. Although Hussein failed to get into the military academy, in 1976 he was appointed by then-President Bakr to the rank of lieutenant general, equivalent to the chief of staff. Three years later, on assuming the presidency, he promoted himself to the rank of field marshal. During the war years, the Iraqi media abounded with descriptions of Hussein as a military genius of the highest order. Through sustained effort, Hussein has created a docile and highly politicized military leadership, vetted and promoted on the principle of personal loyalty and kinship rather than on professional excellence. Consequently, when the Iran-Iraq war broke out, the military was no more courageous than the politicians, challenging neither Hussein's war strategy nor his conduct of war operations.

Hussein's strategy of limited war made little military sense. Instead of dealing a mortal blow to the Iranian army and trying to topple the revolutionary regime in Teheran,

Hussein called for a quick, limited campaign, reasoning that it would bring the clerics back to their senses without painting them into a corner. At the same time, Hussein failed to grasp the operational requirements of such a campaign. Instead of allowing the army to advance until its momentum was exhausted, Hussein ordered it to halt only a week after the outbreak of hostilities, while it was still advancing. The decision saved the Iranian army from a decisive defeat, and gave Teheran time to reorganize and regroup. It also devastated the morale of the Iraqi army, and hence its combat performance.

Using the Revolutionary Command Council as his personal headquarters. Hussein maintained tight control of war operations. This was clearly demonstrated by the inflexibility and lack of initiative on the part of Iraq's field commanders. Battalion and brigade commanders were unwilling to make independent decisions in rapidly changing battlefield situations, referring back to division or corps headquarters, which in turn approached the highest command in Baghdad.

The first rumblings of discontent from the military came in autumn 1982, when Iraq was already defending its own territory against Iran's human-wave attacks. Hussein responded by executing some three-hundred high-ranking officers, along with a small number of party officials; others were purged. It was reported that Hussein himself executed an officer who ordered a tactical retreat. According to the story, the hapless officer was thrown it front of his Commander in Chief, who calmly drew his pistol and shot the man in the head. Word of this decisive act, which occurred at about the same time that Hussein was said to have murdered his Minister of Health, sent a clear signal to the military.

Not until 1996—when, after an impressive series of Iranian victories, the specter of defeat loomed larger than ever—did the officer corps dare to challenge the Commander in Chief. With the Iranian army at the gates of Basra, the second-most important city in Iraq, the military leadership rose up—demanding not political power or the overthrow of the leader who had divided, intimidated, and battered it for nearly two decades, but simply the freedom to run the war according to its best judgment.

This exceptional demonstration of resolve saved Iraq from disaster. Threatened by military defeat, Hussein grudgingly gave into his generals (though not without instantly purging their ranks). His concession led to a series of Iraqi successes that culminated in Teheran's agreement to a cease-fire after eight years of fighting.

During this period, the balance of power between Hussein and his military was shifting decisively. When General Rashid gave his ill-timed interviews to the Kuwaiti press, an outraged Hussein ordered his kinsman (the general's daughter was at the time married to Hussein's younger son, Kusay) to report back to Baghdad immediately. Well aware of what the order meant, Rashid's officers transmitted a warning to Hussein, implying that they would refuse to prosecute the war should anything happen to their commander. On arriving at the presidential palace, Rashid was decorated by a beaming Hussein, who deferred vengeance for later.

The end of the Iran-Iraq war in the summer of 1988 ushered in a new stage in Hussein's relations with the military. First, the belief that lying low and avoiding any taint of political activity provided some insurance against the whims of the regime was shattered by the purges of the late war years. Second, Hussein's concessions to the military during the war proved that even he was not invincible. This combination of fear and hope accounts for the growing number of reported coup attempts in the postwar era, the most recent taking place just before the occupation of Kuwait.

Thus far, Hussein has successfully kept his officers at bay. However, his position is not as unassailable as it was in the mid-1980's. Indeed, the invasion of Kuwait can be seen as an act of weakness. In order to wield absolute power once again, the Iraqi president desperately needed a spectacular achievement. Kuwait offered an ideal opportunity. Its occupation could engage the military ranks in a riskless venture abroad, thus satisfying their yearning for national gratitude while keeping them at a safe distance from Baghdad, and it could lift Hussein's national prestige by positioning him as the liberator of an integral part of Iraq, torn away by Western colonialists. By seizing Kuwait's financial assets, Hussein hoped to slash Iraq's foreign debt and launch the ambitious reconstruction programs he promised his people in the wake of the war. Last but not least, the occupation of Kuwait would make Iraq the dominant regional power and give it a decisive say in the world oil market. In short, a new Babylon would emerge in the Middle East, ruled by a latter-day Nebuchadnezzar.

In September 1980, Hussein drew his country into what he believed would be a brief campaign. He found himself engaged in the longest and bloodiest conflict of the postwar era. A decade later, he has sent his armies on what promised to be a costless walkover, only to put his country on a collision course with the entire international community.

JANINE DI GIOVANNI

The Enemy of Our Enemy

AHMED CHALABI, a Shiite Muslim from a prominent Baghdad family, is by turns haughty and brooding, princely and strangely preoccupied. In the cold weather, he goes about London in a goatskin robe, which he likes to flick grandly behind him, and Gore-Tex hiking boots. But while he may look like some tribal elder who wandered down from the hills (in trendy shoes), he holds a Ph.D. in mathematics from the University of Chicago and is fluent in several languages. He is also the closest thing either the Clinton administration or its Republican opponents have to a strategy for replacing the failed policy of containing Saddam Hussein.

JANINE DI GIOVANNI *is a National Magazine Award winner who covers the Middle East, Chechnya, Algeria, Rwanda, and East Timor. She is the author of* The Quick and the Dead: Under Siege in Sarajevo. *This piece originally appeared in 2000 in the* New York Times.

Chalabi, fifty-five, is the

head of the Iraqi National Congress, the once and, for now, future guiding body of the Iraqi opposition to Saddam Hussein. Having been pushed aside early last year, Chalabi managed to reclaim his leadership position at a general assembly of the I.N.C. in New York this fall. And that, it bears mentioning, was no easy task. The three-hundred-plus delegates who came from Britain, Lebanon, Syria, Turkey, Iraq, Jordan, Saudi Arabia, Iran, Turkey, and Canada shared little but a fissiparous history of backstabbing and mistrust. In truth, they gathered only to prove to their American patrons that they were still collectively committed to overthrowing the only person they loathe more than one another—the devil in Baghdad.

In the dimly lighted corridors of a Manhattan hotel, men in flowing robes and headdresses stood next to men in cheap shiny suits, whispering in Arabic like schoolchildren. "No one likes each other," sighed one delegate who showed me around. There were other problems. Hamid al-Bayati, a representative of the Supreme Council for Islamic Revolution in Iraq, withdrew from the assembly. Massoud Barzani, president of the Kurdish Democratic Congress, never arrived.

The delegates chose to ignore the slights and continue. They distributed "Free Iraq" T-shirts and squabbled. They argued throughout the weekend—over the buffet dinner, over mint tea, and over the fax machine spewing out messages from across the world. Somehow, by dawn on Monday morning, they managed to conclude the general assembly by electing a new seven-man leadership, and with a minimal amount of blood on the floor. But not before Ahmed Chalabi had walked out several times in disgust. "It was not a pretty sight," one delegate said. "They threw shoes at each other. I couldn't believe it. They took off their shoes and threw them at each other."

They threw shoes because they are desperate. With Washington acting as midwife, the organization is now under serious pressure to get results. With an impending presidential election—and with Saddam now exercising virtual veto power on United Nations weapons inspectors—the Democrats are growing increasingly anxious to have something, anything, they can plausibly hold up as a proactive Iraq policy.

The Republicans, eager to pre-empt the Democrats, are claiming it was their idea to back the I.N.C. and that they had to push the administration into getting behind it. With both parties competing to be its patron, the organization would seem to be well positioned to make good on its longstanding promise of fomenting a revolution from below. And yet it doesn't seem any closer now to that goal than it did eight years ago, when it was formed in the wake of the Persian Gulf War. While Congress appropriated $97 million to bankroll the seven principal opposition groups, the money has remained in Washington as the groups have jockeyed for power.

The power struggle seems to be in abeyance, but that still leaves the I.N.C. with one major problem: it hasn't figured out a way to outsmart its nemesis, a ruthless dictator who has faced down more than one attempted revolution or coup in his years in power. "Saddam kills anyone he doesn't trust," says one observer. "He squashes opposition like a bug."

In its short and painful life, the Iraqi National Congress has done little to inspire confidence that it could ever serve as the linchpin for American policy. Only now can it be said to be coming of age, and at that, very slowly. The formal seven-man presidency includes representatives of all the major factions. Chalabi was given no official title, but he is acknowledged to be acting in a presiding role.

It is a perplexing group. Each faction appears to have its own agenda: the Kurds, for instance, have the issue of nationalism; the monarchists want to see a royal return; the Islamic groups are paralyzed by infighting. Yet all now protest their undying solidarity. "All Iraqi opposition groups are united on the need to get rid of Saddam," Chalabi insists. "We all want the same thing. A democratic Iraq."

Adds Sharif Au Bin al-Hussein, the forty-three-year-old leader of the Constitutional Monarchy Party: "We have a common goal and a common strategy. It's not about power, it's about unity of Iraqi opposition." This was echoed (cautiously) by the Kurdish leader Jalal Talabani and the others.

"What is important now," one delegate said heatedly, "is getting rid of Saddam. Together."

Chalabi is insistent that this time the opposition will get it right. "Look, we don't want to get a bunch of guns and go blazing into the sunshine," Chalabi said. "We are going to work with careful steps to prepare with the U.S. so that our forces are ready."

For veteran I.N.C.-watchers, "blazing into the sunshine" is a not-so-veiled reference to the group's Waterloo—the 1996 debacle in Irbil, a town in northern Iraq that served as its base of operations before it was leveled by Saddam's tanks. For the I.N.C., Irbil is a gaping, deep wound that just won't heal. "You ask why we don't have an army, why we aren't preparing actively?" asks Aras Habib, the organization's operations chief. "We had an army. We had a good army. We had weapons. We were fighters. It was destroyed in Irbil."

The Iraqi National Congress was born in 1992, in the wake of the Persian Gulf War, with Chalabi as its democratically elected president. Its operatives lobbied diplomats, opened a human rights office, and developed military, political and intelligence operations, largely operating out of Irbil. What they did not do is establish a financial infrastructure or a real plan to overthrow Saddam. Vagueness has always been the I.N.C.'s downfall.

The closest thing to a plan was Chalabi's "enclave" or "three city" strategy. "I always refused to subscribe to the American policy of containment," he says. "My strategy was to construct an enclave and to unite all the opposition groups, including the Kurds, to form an alliance."

Chalabi's plan was to capture Kirkuk and Mosul, the leading cities in the north of Iraq, and Basra, the main southern city, and slowly squeeze the life out of Saddam's regime. "He believed that the Iraqis themselves have the willingness to rise up against Saddam," says Zaab Sethna, an I.N.C. adviser who sees Chalabi more as a visionary than as a naïf. "But this could only be done if the I.N.C. built up its strength in the north and the south by luring defectors and acquiring arms."

Whether ultimately feasible or not, the plan suffered from two major and, as it turned out, fatal flaws. First, it demanded the cooperation of the two main Kurdish factions—the Kurdish Democratic Party (K.D.P.) and the Patriotic Union of Kurdistan (P.U.K.)—which had a long history of bloody feuds. "To think one could unite the Kurds under one anti-Saddam banner when they had historically been incapable of uniting themselves was overly optimistic," says Patrick Bishop, a Paris-based Middle East specialist. "Over the years, the main Kurdish groups have shown themselves capable of getting in bed with the devil if they felt it suited their interest."

Second, the plan assumed the full cooperation of the Central Intelligence Agency, which had been trying for years to oust Saddam. But the C.I.A. didn't buy into Chalabi's strategy, insisting that the dictator would succumb only to a coup.

Chalabi, believing the regime would topple under sustained pressure and counting on American support, went ahead with plans to attack Kirkuk and Mosul. By the summer of 1996, he says, he had a C.I.A.-trained army of more than one-thousand and a highly effective intelligence operation.

But on the night of August 31, 1996, Chalabi's plans were blasted into the thin desert air. "I was sitting in a meeting at the American Embassy in London between the P.U.K. and the K.D.P.," he says, "when Saddam's tanks crept up on the outskirts of Irbil." A bitter tone creeps into his voice. "We waited for air support, but it never arrived."

"Apparently, it was gruesome," Sethna recalls. "Fighters were calling from the satellite phones. They could see the tanks in the distance, and they kept calling and calling for help but no one came." Saddam had been invited in by Massoud Barzani, the Kurdish Democratic Party leader, who saw a way to eliminate both the Iraqi National Congress and the Patriotic Union of Kurdistan in one treacherous move. The C.I.A., fearing another debacle like the Bay of Pigs, refused to help. Hundreds of I.N.C. men were executed, and thousands more fled to Turkey.

Chalabi's critics scoffed at the idea that the I.N.C. could ever seriously challenge Saddam's Republican Guard, eighty-thousand strong, and his superior weaponry. They also dismissed his claims about his intelligence network and disparaged him as a leader. But the debate was moot by the morning of September 1, when, for all practical purposes, the Iraqi National Congress ceased to exist.

Among the issues raised against Chalabi—and there are many, including a conviction for embezzlement—is the constant refrain that he is not a "man of the people" and will never win the allegiance of his diverse and fractious supporters. There is some truth to this. Chalabi was indeed reared like a little prince until the monarchy under King Faisal II was overthrown by a group of officers in 1958.

His family was wealthy, powerful, and renowned. His father, Abdul Hadi, was a cabinet minister and later the president of the senate. His grandfather, Abdul Hussein, was a member of Iraq's first Parliament, a cabinet minister nine different times. His mother held political salons at their grand house with its lush, jasmine-scented gardens, where young Ahmed listened attentively.

But his world began to come apart after the 1958 coup. The real threat was not from the new military rulers but from the Baath Party, a vaguely socialist and nationalist group dedicated to overthrowing what its members saw as a hopelessly corrupt regime in thrall to the colonialist powers. The Baathists had their first taste of power in 1963, in a coup led by General Abdul Salam Arif.

Recognizing the threat the Baath Party posed to his family, Chalabi, then nineteen and a student at the Massachusetts Institute of Technology, plotted its overthrow with a group of disgruntled army officers in Beirut. "I was determined to claim my life back in Iraq," he says. He failed, although General Arif subsequently banished his former partners.

But in 1968, a second Baath coup succeeded, with the help of a young deputy named Saddam Hussein. By 1979, he was president.

"The day in 1968 that I got the news of Saddam," says Chalabi, who by then was a graduate student at the University of Chicago, "I rushed through my Ph.D. exams in mathematics and caught a plane to Teheran. I had an idea. I knew the Kurdish leaders. And the only way to drive Saddam from power was to unite them."

This was no easier in 1968 than in 1996—or now. It meant drawing together warring factions: the K.D.P., then led by Massoud Barzani's father, Mustafa, and its rival, the P.U.K., under Jalal Talabani. "The strategy is the same one I brought back twenty years later," when the I.N.C. was born, he says. It came to naught, of course, and by 1969, the Chalabi dynasty in Iraq had disappeared (his family compound now houses the Indian Embassy), its members dispersed throughout the Middle East, America, and Europe.

The newly invigorated I.N.C. has temporarily shelved the three-city plan. Its more modest goal now is simply to get off the ground: setting up bank accounts, re-establishing contacts in Iraq. Mostly, says Daniel Byman, a Middle East expert at the Rand Corporation, they are waiting, waiting "for a lucky break so they can fill in the gap. I honestly don't think they know what that is. Maybe Saddam will take a lucky bullet. Maybe there will be a change in government and they will step in. That seems to be their plan."

But many who follow the I.N.C. detect another old strategy—revolution from below. They say the organization's leaders still fantasize about getting a chunk of American money, establishing a beachhead in Iraq, and inspiring thousands of disgruntled soldiers and millions of frustrated people to rise up and slay the tyrant. "The regime topples," as one analyst says, "and they then get alongside the people."

But to Byman and many others that is wishful thinking. "In real life that doesn't happen," he says. "We would be in the same situation as the Bay of Pigs. Just watching guys get killed, or we go in and take on Saddam ourselves. It's a pathetic military plan." The Pentagon has already warned the I.N.C. that it will not bail it out if it gets into another Irbil-like mess.

Chalabi, back in London, admits that he is "not happy with the pace that things are moving." In December, a State Department contract that provided the I.N.C. with office space and supplies ran out. An answering service now takes the calls, and Chalabi is harder to pin down. "We are waiting for the grant, the money appropriated from Congress to arrive," Chalabi explains, once found, in his car driving to yet another leadership meeting. Arabic music blasts in the background, and he sounds frustrated.

But he also insists that the organization has a coherent plan and that last year was a turning point. "We have several projects," he says. The first one is comprehensible: setting up a media operation with satellite TV and radio broadcasts into Iraq to break Saddam's monopoly. "He controls the nerve center of the media," Chalabi says. "You can't communicate with people without him finding out; you can't move people."

The second plan is murkier. "It involves training," Chalabi says. "For instance, how to deal with large population movements—if Saddam attacks and people have to flee. How do we feed them, where do they go." Then he lowers his voice and opens up more. "Basically, we are training people inside and outside the country who will operate things in the process of getting rid of Saddam."

That strategy also involves more I.N.C. work directly inside Iraq. "We are working there," Chalabi claims. "The one difference is that we have moved focus from the north to the south and west of the country, even inside of Baghdad." The north of the country, for the moment, is left alone. "The Kurds," he says, "are enjoying relative security and we are concentrating on other parts of the country." Given the I.N.C.'s history with the Kurds, it seems a wise decision.

Meanwhile, Saddam is widely believed to have taken advantage of a year free of United Nations weapons inspectors to resume development of chemical, nuclear, and biological weapons. While he is not directly threatened by outside forces, other than the occasional bombing raid by allied warplanes, he is said to be paranoid about internal threats. In November, according to intelligence reports, he called in his military commanders for consultations in small groups—an indication of growing suspicion.

Whether he was concerned about the I.N.C. or some other, undetected threat is debatable. "There are signs," says one academic analyst. "Saddam was very nervous about the New York meeting." But there are also signs that he hardly noticed it. "If he was worried, the Iraqi press wouldn't be writing about it in their newspapers," another analyst says. "They are certainly not writing about what is happening in the south. Now that would be damaging to Saddam."

One thing has emerged from New York: the I.N.C. has been granted a last opportunity to grow up and become a serious player. "The October summit was like crossing the Rubicon," admits one State Department official, who said he had more faith in the opposition than ever before. There is also the growing Congressional support, particularly among Republicans looking to highlight the failed Clinton policy.

Ahmed Chalabi works hard on his Washington connections. Senators Trent Lott, Joseph Lieberman, and Bob Kerrey have consistently backed him, and new friends like Senator Sam Brownback and David Scheffer, the United States ambassador at large for war crimes, all pledged their support at the New York meeting. Even Thomas Pickering, the under secretary for political affairs, offered "protection and help" for opposition groups working toward a regime change, and showed up for the conclusion of the I.N.C. general assembly.

But how seriously does Washington really take Chalabi and his organization? So far, the support seems to be a mile wide and an inch deep. "The I.N.C. has a lot of support because Congress is full of a lot of posturing idiots who couldn't find Iraq on the map and don't know anything about foreign policy," says one critic. "They just know something has to change."

But Daniel Byman points out that the I.N.C. has taken two major steps in the last year. "One is their change in leadership, which remedies some of their problems," he says. "The other is that they've moved away from past grandiose schemes like marching on Baghdad to addressing basic organizational steps that they avoided for too long." However, Byman still has his doubts about the fundamental differences within the coalition. "They all agree that Saddam should go," he frets, "but what else they agree on, I'm not sure."

The Clinton administration is equally unsure about Chalabi, both for his personality quirks and for his history.

For a time last year, it even seemed as if the White House would rather see Saddam in Baghdad than Chalabi. "They were down on Ahmed because of Jordan," says one Washington observer. (In 1989, Chalabi was indicted for embezzling millions from a Jordanian bank he founded in the 1970s. He was eventually convicted in absentia.) Another blow came in 1998 when General Anthony Zinni, commander of the American forces in the Persian Gulf, bluntly told Congress that the opposition groups "have little, if any, viability."

But the skepticism has quieted down, whether for cynical reasons, a growing sense of respect for the I.N.C., or plain desperation. "The Saddam regime has got to go," says one senior State Department official. "We crossed that bridge last year. But what is different now is the opposition. Their recriminations have subsided. They're watching each other, watching Washington. They're more sober."

Exactly how Chalabi and his men are going to pull off a stunt like getting rid of Saddam Hussein, when the international forces during the Gulf War could not, remains to be seen. For now, the Iraqi National Congress appears to be starting with basic organizational issues that should have been addressed a decade ago. "They're asking how broad a coalition they can get, and how they can share resources and leadership," says Byman. "It has been a good year because they are sitting down and talking, but that's the first step in one-hundred and they still have ninety-nine to go."

DAVID ROSE

The Arsenal of Terror

JANUARY 2000: a chilly afternoon in Baghdad. At the downtown headquarters of Iraq's Military Industrial Commission, the body responsible for arms development and purchase, its then chairman, General Amer al-Saadi gathered thirteen government officials around the boardroom table: scientists, soldiers, spies. More than a year had passed since the Iraqi president, Saddam Hussein, expelled the inspectors from the United Nations Special Commission (UNSCOM), the U.N. program designed to prevent Iraq from acquiring weapons of mass destruction. "Now we're a free country again," al-Saadi said. "We can do whatever we wish. We want you to work with full force, and you'll be in a race against time.

DAVID ROSE
is an author and world explorer. He is a contributing editor at Vanity Fair *where he has written extensively on the problems afflicting the Middle East and specifically the unique role Iraq plays in the conflict. This piece was originally appeared in* Vanity Fair *in 2000.*

You have to win this race. Everything you need, material or logistic, is available to you."

Al-Saadi, a plump, white-haired man in his early sixties, spoke for three hours. The course of the race, he said, was still unknown. Its finish line, however, was clearly fixed. What al-Saadi called "the Motherland" would win if those in the room reached their goal—a new-generation long-range ballistic-missile system, equipped to deliver chemical, biological, and eventually nuclear warheads.

Twenty-six months after al-Saadi's address, in March 2002, a man who says he was present—a man who has since escaped Iraq—is in a hotel in a Middle Eastern capital describing it for *Vanity Fair*.

This defector has disclosed new details of Iraq's programs for building missiles and weapons of mass destruction. Iraq is close, he says, to achieving a long-range missile capable of hitting the capitals of Turkey, Egypt, Cyprus, Iran, and Saudi Arabia. He has supplied new information about how the country has built a network of front companies, controlled by its intelligence service, to evade Western sanctions, and identified seven sites where chemical and biological weapons are designed, manufactured, and tested, and an eighth where nuclear weapons are again being developed. With evident pride, he describes the success of his scheme to build a fleet of virtually undetectable mobile biological weapons trucks, indistinguishable in appearance from the vehicles used to carry chilled or frozen food.

On a map he traces the course of four specially reinforced roadways, in all about five-hundred miles in length, on which Iraq can turn its existing missiles into moving targets firing them from mobile launchers in the event of war. The defector also describes Iraq's support for Hamas, the Palestinian terrorist group responsible for suicide bombings in Israel, and his journey to Africa to buy highly toxic radioactive material with which to build a radiological bomb.

In the weeks before our interviews, this man, who left Iraq a year and a half ago, was debriefed in at least four lengthy sessions by U.S. officials from the Defense Intelligence Agency. He is hoping to find sanctuary for himself and his family. Meanwhile, *Vanity Fair* has copied and translated some of the documentation he supplied to his U.S. interrogators. It includes the paperwork produced to establish his cover as a journalist and a twenty-two-page report on military radar systems from the organization to which he once belonged—Iraq's security and intelligence service, the Mukhabarat.

Although *Vanity Fair* cannot independently verify all the defector's claims, experts on Iraq say they are consistent with other established information and appear to be credible. Charles Duelfer, the former deputy chairman of the UNSCOM mission in Iraq, who continues to monitor the region at the Center for Strategic and International Studies in Washington, has reviewed all the defector's testimony at the request of *Vanity Fair*. He says, "I haven't found anything to make me disbelieve him. What he describes is consistent with what we know about how Iraq operates, both in terms of building weapons of mass destruction, and in terms of its efforts to procure the necessary equipment and materials. His evidence tells us that Iraq's weapons-of-mass-destruction program has only accelerated since UNSCOM was expelled from the country in 1998."

A tall, slim man in his late thirties, the defector says he was trusted with sensitive positions early in his Mukhabarat career. Although an interpreter is present to ensure accuracy throughout our interviews, he speaks passable English, and often answers my questions without waiting for their Arabic translation. After he graduated from Baghdad's School of National Security in 1986, he says, his first job was with the division responsible for government ministers' security—in the sense not of providing them with personal protection, but of keeping them under surveillance for the least sign of dissent. In 1992, he says, he was transferred to what Iraq called the Directorate for Secret Organizations and Relations—the department which, among other functions, provided support and training for terrorists from abroad.

There were two foreign groups for which he was personally responsible, he says. The first was the Iranian opposition force, the Mujahideen e-Khalq, which during the 1980s maintained at least twenty-thousand fighters inside Iraq, where it helped suppress the 1991 Shiite uprising. The second was the Popular Front for the Liberation of Palestine, which carried out a long string of murders and hijackings up until the early 1990s. Its founder, George Habash, was a visitor to Baghdad, the defector tells me, and at least fifty of his colleagues lived there. However, by the early 1990s, the Popular Front's place in the terrorist pantheon was being usurped by a still more deadly formation—Hamas, perfecters of suicide bombing.

Evidence of links between Iraq and Hamas has surfaced before. It is known that Saddam sends $10,000 to the family of each "martyr" who kills himself in a suicide attack. In an official communiqué, Hamas refers to "brotherly Iraq," and during the lull in Palestinian-Israeli violence that followed the 1993 Oslo peace accords, Hamas threatened to kill civilians in Israel if the U.S. made any move against Iraq. The defector's testimony reveals the true depth of the Iraq-Hamas connection. It places Iraq squarely on the front line of President Bush's war on international terrorism: even without the added factor of weapons of mass destruction, this might be held to justify a U.S. attack.

Hamas had a subdepartment all its own in the foreigners' directorate, he says, and throughout the time he worked there, the Mukhabarat provided Hamas with a full-time office in the Karrada Dakhil district of Baghdad. A stream of Hamas fighters learned skills in Iraq, with successive classes of between five and thirty students trained at the Salman Pak terrorist camp, south of Baghdad, and at a similar facility in the Diyala district of northeastern Iraq. In those locations, in addition to the normal curriculum of sabotage, assassination, and train and airplane hijackings, a fellow Mukhabarat officer gave Hamas members instruction in a further specialty: suicide bombing. "Many weapons were being supplied to Hamas," the defector says, "guns, ammunition both heavy and light, detonators, and explosives. It was Iraq which trained Hamas in how to make bombs."

The defector says he was ordered to embark on a very different kind of mission in October 1994. Before the Gulf War, Iraq had come close to building an atomic bomb: under a fast-track scheme Saddam had sponsored, it would have rushed out a crude device using fuel from its nuclear reactors. In his book *Saddam's Bombmaker*, published in 2000, Khidhir Hamza, Iraq's former nuclear-program chief, states that while this bomb would have been too heavy for a missile warhead, it could have been used "for a demonstration test, or, as we discovered to our horror, Saddam's plan to drop one unannounced on Israel." But Iraq's Gulf War defeat and the consequent imposition of the UNSCOM inspectors caused a series of reverses. The United States destroyed Iraq's last uranium reactor in 1991.

The defector's 1994 mission was apparently undertaken to help remedy this deficit. He shows me his passport: the stamps confirm he left Iraq for Amman, the capital of neighboring Jordan, on October 17, 1994. In all, he says, there were three in his party: himself, a Mukhabarat colleague, and a scientist.

In Amman, the embassy liaison officer, a Mukhabarat operative, gave the three men new passports. They traveled to Khartoum, the capital of Sudan, and changed passports again: now they were supposedly businessmen from the United Arab Emirates. Next stop, by the Italian airline Alitalia, was Rome. From there they flew to Algiers, and thence, finally, to Dar es Salaam, Tanzania.

Joined there by more Iraqis, they drove into the bush to an isolated house, where they were met by five Eastern Europeans Russians, the defector believes, or possible Ukrainians. "They had a trunk made of heavy metal, about a meter long, so heavy they could barely lift it. They had a sports bag and took out gloves, face masks which were like gas masks, and a small electronic gadget. They opened the trunk, and the scientist bent over it. Inside were what looked like pieces of black rock, glittery." Some were the size and shape of fingers; others looked like lumps of coal. The scientist examined them with a handheld device. The defector says that unlike a Geiger counter, this made a bleeping sound when placed near the material. Satisfied, the scientist ordered that the trunk be resealed. He treated his hands, his face, and the trunk with decontaminants, the defector recalls. One of his colleagues opened his briefcase. Inside were neat stacks of $100 bills. He handed the case to the Eastern Europeans.

The defector admits he is no technician, and some nuclear experts are skeptical of certain details in his account. But according to the same experts, the "fingers" of black material sounds like a description of spent reactor fuel rods cut into sections which could be used to build a "dirty," radiological bomb—a conventional explosive surrounded by a layer of radioactive material, designed to spew across a wide area. Charles Dueller, the former

UNSCOM deputy chairman, adds, "The defector's description is consistent with what we know about Iraq's attempt to continue its nuclear program. Iraq has demonstrated it is interested in building dirty weapons of this kind." Iraq unsuccessfully tested at least one such bomb in 1987–88, in the closing stages of the Iran-Iraq War.

Far easier to build than a full-fledged nuclear device, a dirty bomb would kill its victims slowly: those who survived the initial blast would be at risk of developing cancers after inhaling or swallowing the radioactive wrapping, which the explosion would reduce to fine particles of dust. A dirty bomb could also be delivered to its target in many ways. A small device might be detonated inside a suitcase or lodged beneath a car; larger bombs could be fired from a missile or dropped from an airplane.

The man seated before me says that, in September 1996, he was promoted and moved to a new posting, attached to a special commercial department of the Military Industrial Commission. Iraq's weapons-development-and-procurement programs were in a state of upheaval. Their former overseer, Hussein Kamel, Saddam's son-in-law and formerly one of his confidants, had fled to the West, where he gave intelligence agencies many damaging details of Iraq's secret programs. Then, apparently feeling homesick, Kamel had unwisely chosen to believe Saddam's promises that all would he forgiven if he would only return. He was murdered together with his father, two brothers, his sister, and her two young children after a long gun battle at a brother's home in Baghdad. Kamel's wife, Saddam's daughter, survived. His mother was killed two years later. Henceforth, weapons acquisition came under the direct control of Saddam and his son Uday.

That summer, this new defector says, the Mukhabarat began to form and operate a network of commercial companies. It had three purposes. The first was to raise currency to buy military hardware abroad through what amounted to a huge money-laundering scam that would take advantage of the U.N's "food for oil" program. Under the program, Iraq is allowed to import a limited range of nonlethal items paid for in kind with oil. The Mukhabarat's firms, which had branches in Iraq, Jordan, and the United Arab Emirates, sold these items—trucks, cars, food, building materials, and electronics, as well as more obscure goods such as spare parts for flour mills. No matter if the people of Iraq were further impoverished as a result: just one of the thousands of individual deals concluded in this way might raise as much as $20 million for arms procurement, the defector says. He gave me a list of ten firms, together with the names of some of their directors and office addresses. He believes they are all still in business. The network is controlled by Saddam's son Uday, who takes a personal commission on every deal. "To import or export anything in Iraq, you need a license from [Uday's office at the Iraqi] Olympic Committee," the defector says.

The companies' second purpose, he says, was smuggling. "Why do you think televisions and refrigerators imported from Jordan go to Iraq via Dubai?" he asks. The reason, he says, is that in a Mukhabarat front-company warehouse in the United Arab Emirates Iraqi agents open their casings and stuff them with items banned under U.N. sanctions, such as fiber-optic cables and electronic components destined for military use. Finally, the front firms were used to buy military equipment and raw materials.

The defector says his job within this network was control and liaison: to watch what the companies were doing and, after collecting shopping lists from the Iraqi military and the Military Industrial Commission, to tell them what to do. "I might be in a meeting with the commission. They'd say they needed missile covers, carbon fiber, supercomputers, missile ignition systems, electronic parts, thermal lenses for radar receivers, fuel for missiles." In flagrant breach of U.N. sanctions, this man and his colleagues would try to ensure that these needs were met.

His cover—what Iraqi spies call their "legend"—was elaborate. The Mukhabarat had established a weekly business newspaper, *al-Iqtisadi*, purely as a way of providing camouflage for its agents' activities. The paper—which is on sale in several Arab countries—is produced by an editorial group in Baghdad. Like most of its supposed journalistic staff, the defector never wrote a word. The paper gave him freedom to travel, a pretext for applying for foreign visas, and a plausible reason for making visits to Iraqi businesses abroad. His letter of credentials, signed by the paper's supposed editor, Muhammad Jafar Dawood, states: "*Al-Iqtisadi* weekly newspaper authorizes [name withheld] to contact Jordanian ministries, companies, and establishments to conduct interviews and write reports and collect subscriptions and commercial advertisements. He is also authorized to receive cash and checks in his name which he endorses and cashes according to official receipts issued by *Al-Iqtisadi* newspaper. We appreciate your assistance to facilitate his mission."

Charles Dueller, the former UNSCOM deputy chief, says the defector's information about front companies is new, credible, and important. Equally significant, in his view, is the defector's testimony about biological weapons. Despite his relatively junior rank—the equivalent of a major—he apparently had access to the most secret parts of Saddam's schemes for mass annihilation. In the summer of 1996 he found himself at a meeting with Dr. Rehab Taha, also known as "Dr. Germ," a female scientist in charge of Iraq's biological weapons. At this time, UNSCOM had not yet been expelled, and he came up with a plan to enable these weapons and development programs to evade detection, then and in the future. "They had the same problem as any stationary facility," the defector says. "I suggested we go for mobile units."

He says he and Dr. Taha wrote a report for Saddam, who rapidly approved it. He organized the purchase of eight heavy Renault trucks from France—a perfectly legal deal carried out through Iraq's Ministry of Commerce. At the secret al-Iskandariyya facility in the Hilla Province, engineers converted them into factories of mass destruction. "They look like meat cars, yogurt cars," he says. "And inside is a laboratory, with incubators for bacteria, microscopes, air-conditioning." It was a good idea, I say grimly. The man beams and says in English, "Thanks a lot!" Yet he got no reward for his ingenuity, he complains. "Had I been a Tikriti [a member of Saddam's tribe, from the area north of Baghdad], I would have been given a new Toyota."

Much worse than mere ingratitude was to come. One day in 1997, he says, he was with a friend, buying a present for his wife, when the store owner, a devout Shiite Muslim, asked him to use his official connections to secure permission for printing a religious newspaper and theological texts. A religious man himself, he saw no political danger in helping out, and he obtained permission from the Ministry of Information. But in the paranoid climate of Iraq, the Mudiryat al-Amn al-A'ma, archrival to the Mukhabarat, believed that the Shiite printing scheme was really a conspiracy to topple Saddam. The defector was one of twenty-nine supposed plotters arrested in September 1998. He says he was tortured and interrogated for the next six months.

He shows me some of the scars. On his left eyelid is a bump where he says the Mudiryat al-Amn al-A'ma's Russian-trained chief torturer, known as "the Shuffler," attached a crocodile-clip electrode. Another was clipped to his genitals. His feet and ankles bear scalpel scars: he says that after puncturing his veins his tormentors used bands to compress his thighs to squeeze the blood from his legs. He says he also endured sexual abuse. For a time, he was held in a cell once occupied by the British journalist Farzad Bazoft, who was executed on trumped-up spying charges in 1990. On the wall, Bazoft had scrawled his name and a warning: DON'T SPEAK. THERE'S A MICROPHONE HIDDEN IN THE WALL.

On several occasions, the defector says, he was tied by his arms in a standing position to the bars of his cell. "You could stay like that for ten, fifteen days, for everything, eating, drinking, and . . . you know." There were psychological techniques: he was shown a video of children aged from five to ten being tortured, with the threat that the same fate might await his own family if he failed to confess.

But he says he didn't confess, and by the middle of March 1999 his interrogators were satisfied he was telling the truth. He spent another three months in much more comfortable conditions, in order to allow him to recover from his injuries, and in July he was released. The Mukhabarat gave him a month's leave. And then, entrusted with the most sensitive tasks of his entire career, he went back to work. Khidhir Hamza, the nuclear scientist, says such treatment is common in Saddam's Iraq: some of his colleagues in the nuclear program also got their jobs back after being tortured. "As long as they find nothing, it's normal," he says. "Maybe they give you some kind of gift to make it up to you."

The regime assumes that brutalizing its servants in this way will keep them loyal through a mixture of greed and fear. "They believe that if you're jailed and you come out clean they can use this as a warning," the defector says. In his case, the worm turned. Freed from jail, he resolved to gather as much information as he could and, when the opportunity arose, to flee.

Before his incarceration, most of his work was concerned with the Mukhabarat front companies' efforts to raise hard currency. Now his focus shifted, and he says he found himself indoctrinated into Iraq's deepest secrets: its attempts to renew its arsenal of weapons of mass destruction, and build a new long-range-missile system with which to deliver them. Before the Gulf War and the arrival of UNSCOM, he says, the facilities which had worked to achieve these ends were concentrated in industrial areas near Baghdad. Now they are widely dispersed. Missile development and testing takes place at the Saad 23 compound at al-Falluja, the defector says, while at Hateen, near al-Musayyib on the road south from Baghdad, Saddam's experts work to develop missile fuel. He lists the other facilities of which he has personal knowledge: electronic guidance systems at al-Harith, in the Kadhimiyya district of Baghdad; missile bodies at Abu Ghraib south of al-Harith; a chemical-weapons factory at Samarra; a biological laboratory at Waziriyya, a suburb of Baghdad; heat-resistant foils and coatings at Ur, the birthplace of the prophet Abraham, in southern Iraq; chemical warheads at al-Musayyib; warhead propellants and covers at the Taiq factory near Taji. Charles Duelfer says the defector's list is "highly credible" and tallies with other information he has in his database, which goes back to the time of UNSCOM's mission.

Like many who have escaped Iraq in the past decade, the

new defector has been brought to the notice of Western intelligence agencies by the Iraqi National Congress, the opposition group funded by the U.S. State Department, which has its head quarters in London. At the end of 2001, it also arranged the defection of Adnan Ihsan Saeed al-Haideri, a building contractor whose firm worked on several Iraq weapons-of-mass-destruction sites, who has now been given refuge in the West. Nabeel Musawi, an Iraqi National Congress agent, says much of the information provided by the two defectors is mutually corroborating. "Neither man knows what the other has told us," he said, "but they're saying the same thing about weapons types and where they're being made."

According to the defector I interviewed, Iraq's renewed attempts to acquire nuclear weapons are concentrated on a project code-named al-Bashir at Fahama, a populous residential area of Baghdad. There, he claims, scientists—some of them foreigners, from countries including Ukraine—examined the possibility of recreating the small, twenty-megawatt "Isis" reactor the destroyed in 1991. The former Iraqi nuclear scientist Khidhir Hamza says that such a reactor, based on the model which enabled India to build its atomic weapons, would produce enough plutonium to build a bomb in approximately two years. However, he believes it unlikely that Iraq would rebuild Isis, saying a more probable route is through using techniques for enriching uranium in which Iraq is already skilled. If it were to acquire the necessary machinery, he says, Iraq already has the knowledge and equipment to use the resultant weapons-grade uranium 235 to produce an atomic bomb.

The defector says that, had he not decided to flee Iraq, his next mission would have been an attempt to procure items for the al-Bashir nuclear project. However, most of his final year as a Mukhabarat officer was spent working on the next generation of Iraqi ballistic missiles. His particular task was a top-secret program, code-named Tammooz.

The terms of U.N. cease-fire resolution 687, which ended the Gulf War, allow Iraq to possess missiles with a maximum range of ninety-three miles—not far enough to hit any significant target outside its borders, with the exception of al-Kuwait, the capital of Kuwait. It is already known that up to forty longer-range "Hussein" missiles, an adapted form of the Scud B system used against Israel during the Gulf War, survived the inspections of the 1990s. The defector says they are hidden around the country on mobile launchers in hangars and on farms with trees to conceal them from aerial surveillance. In the event of war, they would be rolled out along the four specially reinforced roads. These he traces on the map: the highway south from Baghdad to al-Hilla, and the roads from al-Hilla to al-Nasiriyya, from Baghdad east to al-Falluja and al-Ramadi, and, in the south, from al-Kut through al-'Amara to Basra. The missiles can be fired "from anywhere on these lines," he says. "The roads are reinforced with rocks under the asphalt, and renewed three times in a twenty-one-month cycle."

However, deadly as a Hussein missile equipped with a biological or nerve-gas warhead might be, its range is limited to about four-hundred miles. And this can be achieved only at a stretch: the unmodified Scud will fly no farther than half this distance. With such a weapon, Iraq can hit Israel, as it proved in 1991, but other targets remain beyond its reach. The new Tammooz system, the defector says, has been designed with an initial range of six-hundred to seven-hundred miles, far enough to hit Riyadh, Saudi Arabia; Ankara in Turkey; Cairo and Alexandria in Egypt; Nicosia in Cyprus; and Teheran, capital of Iraq's historic enemy, Iran. Later models may extend this by another five-hundred miles—far enough to reach targets across a swath of southern Europe.

By the summer of 2000, the defector says, the Tammooz project was about halfway complete. The first and second stages of the rocket had been built and tested, using steel and carbon fiber imported illegally through the Mukhabarat's front-company web. If Iraq had managed to acquire the supplies it needed, he says, it might have been ready to test a finished missile by the middle of 2001. Traveling via Amman, using his journalistic cover, the defector arrived in Dubai on a mission designed to achieve that end on August 18, 2000. His assignment there was to make all the necessary arrangements for a visit he was scheduled to pay later that month with four Iraqi scientists to Beijing, China, in order to try to buy the outstanding Tammooz components.

In Dubai, he met his Mukhabarat contact, who took

him to the Hotel Inter-Continental Dubai. An hour after checking in, he departed. And then he disappeared.

The defector gazes out the window, then holds his head in his hands. Sometimes his fear is palpable. Did I think he had done the right thing by defecting? he asks. "I'm walking a way I don't know where," he says. "Maybe my road is dangerous." He sighs. "Maybe somebody will save me." At the time of this writing, the opposition Iraqi National Congress is working to rescue members of his family who remain inside Iraq. "I trust my friends in the I.N.C.," he says, "but I'm so alone here."

It was the Iraqi National Congress that organized my interview with this defector—just as it had introduced me in Beirut to the former terrorist trainer Abu Zeinab al-Qurairy, whose story was published in this magazine's February 2002 issue. As I have come to know its operatives across the Middle East, it seems to me they resemble nothing so much as the Underground Railroad, the clandestine network which rescued slaves from the American South before the Civil War. In Washington, State Department officials have criticized the Iraqi National Congress, suggesting it amounts to little more than a bunch of pampered exiles with no real presence or support in Iraq and the surrounding region. My own dealings with it make me question that view. My impression is of a highly organized and motivated group that is able to cross borders to retrieve documents and human beings without detection—and with a network of safe houses, agents, and sympathizers inside Iraq who are prepared to run considerable risks.

As the defector and I spoke, over two long days in March 2002, the debate in the West on what, if anything, to do about Iraq and Saddam Hussein was feverish. Once President Bush had described Iraq as part of an "axis of evil" in his State of the Union address, some kind of intervention seemed inevitable. At the same time, there were powerful voices urging restraint: in the liberal media; in the capitals of Europe; in the State Department and C.I.A.

The defector's information only intensifies the dilemma posed by the persistence of Saddam Hussein. This account of the ease with which Iraq appears to have evaded U.N. sanctions to date does not make one confident that the so-called smart sanctions now being proposed as a means of curbing Saddam's military ambition are any more likely to be effective. At the same time, Saddam's alleged willingness to use a nuclear weapon against Israel before the invasion of Kuwait suggests that the global strategic threat that his possession of weapons of mass destruction represents is not theoretical, but real.

But how far have the Tammooz missile and other programs progressed? How effective are his chemical and biological weapons? How ready are his regime's servants to activate a strategy that might see the Middle East afflicted with biblical destruction in the event of a U.S. attack? On an accurate Western assessment of such questions much may depend.

In a guarded hangar at Saddam International Airport, according to the defector, Hussein keeps a private jet and helicopter in constant readiness: their purpose is to facilitate his flight from Baghdad when the day of reckoning comes. It remains to be seen, assuming he can find someplace willing to let him land, whether he will choose to use that option or to burn in the fire which may now be very near.

HUGH POPE

Culture Change in Iraq

LOOKING AT THE photographs from my last trip to Iraq—crowds hurling insults at George Bush and praising Saddam Hussein—I was shocked by what they revealed. I couldn't see joy or excitement, anger or hatred. There was only a stress so acute that it froze people's faces into unhappy masks, like those used in ancient Greek tragedies.

HUGH POPE *runs the new bureau in Istanbul for the* Wall Street Journal, *reporting on Turkey, and Central Asia. He is the author of* Turkey Unveiled *and has reported for* Vie Independent, The Los Angeles Times, *the BBC, and Reuters. This piece was written in 2002*

The photos showed that most ordinary Iraqis can't be expected to have a real answer to the oft-repeated questions about Iraq: Do Iraqis want to rise up against Saddam Hussein? And: Will the Iraqis resist or welcome an American invasion? Exhaustion, ignorance and, above all, fear—of both oppression and the possibility of another war—are just too great.

Last week, the world caught a glimpse of what can happen when that kind of stress breaks out into the open. Mr. Hussein's decision to give amnesty to thousands of prisoners—a traditional prerogative of Middle Eastern rulers and which last occurred on a smaller scale in Iraq in 1995—provoked a frenzy, in which crowds broke into the main jail and several prisoners were killed in the crush. There also were unprecedented protests outside Iraqi secret-police headquarters by relatives seeking information about the thousands who have disappeared.

The upheaval is part of a more subtle change in the atmosphere in Baghdad from even a month ago. Iraqis' initial shocked rejection of the idea of an American invasion is giving way to an expectation of change, a hope for an end to the crippling past twelve years of sanctions, power cuts, and isolation. Everyone is paying attention to shortwave radios. Many listened live to Mr. Bush's October 7 speech in which he methodically listed the dangers of Mr. Hussein's regime. Iraqis, however, heard only Mr. Bush's words that an invasion wasn't imminent.

That's not to say that ordinary Iraqis are eager to host the Americans. Many still appear sincere in saying that they feel solidarity with their leader, that they loathe America's Middle East policies, and that they blame Washington for the often cruel and fatal consequences of United Nations sanctions. Few Iraqis wanted to defend their leader's 1990 invasion of Kuwait; this time around, their own homes could be the battlefield.

But Iraqis are for the first time considering what an American ouster of Saddam Hussein might mean, and many thoughtful people in Baghdad are reaching some sober conclusions. Changing the character of the regime, whether engineered by the U.S. or by Mr. Hussein himself, will have to be managed as delicately as a diver coming up from the deep. The reality, many Iraqis say, is that the country can be ruled only by Mr. Hussein's brand of toughness. A sudden release from decades of frustration could trigger a popular explosion against Iraq's former masters that could make the country ungovernable for months, if not years.

This *fin de regime* atmosphere has in a sense been helped from the top. An Iraqi who knows about such things says the secret police received orders as long as eighteen months ago not to arrest people simply for speaking against the regime. Over the past year, Internet cafés have allowed a few Iraqis to read mainstream news sites, although usage is monitored and e-mails are counted one by one. Foreign reporters are no longer openly followed, possibly because there are quite enough plainclothes policemen already in the streets. We are free to meet friends and wander around Baghdad.

Then there is the not infrequent sound of the new, American-sponsored Radio Sawa on car radios in Baghdad and Basra. Mr. Hussein's regime knows the danger from the slick, apolitical mix of Western and Arabic popular music, and has started trying to jam the station.

Ordinary people are more eager to signal their rejection of the status quo, either with hand gestures, sighs of assent to pointed questions, and a rolling of the eyes out of sight of the government minder. Once-banned dollars are now openly taken. Iraqis who would not talk about such things to strangers reveal black periods of imprisonment, hatred of the regime or the simple sentiment that Mr. Hussein, in one man's words, "had made enough trouble for us and should go now." In the boisterous open-outcry dollar market of Baghdad's Struggle Street, traders became so outspoken that a government minder became nervous and asked me to leave.

Even Iraqi officials seem different. One was clearly being ironic as he wearily shook his fist and intoned, "we shall fight until the end." Another admitted that the constant life of half-truths has driven him to depression and hard drinking, and has fueled his desire to leave the country. A third, on hearing that Saddam Hussein won 100 percent of the vote in the recent referendum, simply started laughing.

One day, I teased an Iraqi worker about Mr. Hussein's constant television presence. She replied that she genuinely loved her leader, and left. But five minutes later she caught up with me again. "If he's not on television every evening," she said, "we'd be worried sick about what had happened to him." Her open face made me believe her at the time. But without a picture or a tape recorder, I will never know for sure whether her voice registered genuine concern, or fear.

Acknowledgments

We gratefully acknowledge all those who gave permission for written material to appear in this book. We have made every effort to trace and contact copyright holders. If an error or omission is brought to our notice we will be pleased to remedy the situation in future editions of this book. For further information, please contact the publisher.

"The View from Mustansiriyah" by Milton Viorst. Copyright © 1987 by Milton Viorst. Reprinted with permission of The Wylie Agency, Inc. Originally appeared in *The New Yorker*, October 12, 1987.

"Babylon" from *The Carpet Wars* by Christopher Kremmer. Copyright © 2002 by Christopher Kremmer. Reprinted by permission of HarperCollins Publishers, Inc.

Excerpt from *Baghdad Sketches* by Freya Stark. Copyright © 2000 by Freya Stark. Reprinted by permission of John Murray Publishers Ltd.

"Cruel Ancestry" from *The Politics of Revenge* by Saïd K. Aburish. Copyright © 2001 by Saïd K. Aburish. Reprinted with permission of Bloomsbury Publishing plc.

"Mob Town" by Michael Kelly. Copyright © 1993 by The New York Times Co. Reprinted by permission.

"Saddam's Inferno" by Paul William Roberts. Copyright © 1996 by *Harper's Magazine*. All rights reserved. Reproduced from the May issue by special permission.

"Always Remember" by Raymond Bonner. Copyright © 1992 by Raymond Bonner. Reprinted by kind permission of the author. Originally appeared in *The New Yorker*, September 28, 1992.

"Baghdad: In the Land Without Weather" from *Baghdad Without A Map* by Tony Horwitz. Copyright © 1991 by Tony Horwitz. Used by permission of Dutton, a division of Penguin Putnam, Inc.

Excerpt from *Out of the Ashes* by Andrew Cockburn and Patrick Cockburn. Copyright © 1999 by Andrew Cockburn and Patrick Cockburn. Reprinted by permission of HarperCollins Publishers, Inc.

"How Saddam Happened" by Christopher Dickey and Evan Thomas. From *Newsweek,* September 23, 2002. Copyright © 2002 by Newsweek, Inc. All rights reserved. Reprinted by permission.

"America, Oil, and Intervention" by Micah L. Sifry. Copyright © 1991 by Micah L. Sifry. Reprinted by kind permission of the author. All rights reserved.

"Politics is a Lethal Game" by Efraim Karsh. Copyright © 1990 by The New York Times Co. Reprinted by permission.

"The Enemy of Our Enemy" by Janine di Giovanni. Copyright © 2000 by The New York Times Co. Reprinted by permission.

"The Arsenal of Terror" by David Rose. Copyright © 2002 by David Rose. Reprinted by kind permission of the author. Originally appeared in *Vanity Fair,* May 2002.

"Reporter's Notebook: To Iraqis, 'Culture Change' Is Crucial" by Hugh Pope. Reprinted by permission of the *Wall Street Journal,* Copyright © 2002 by Dow Jones & Company, Inc. All Rights Reserved Worldwide. License number 622231394519.